# ANGER MANAGEMENT

## PREVENTION

## UNDERSTANDING

## RESOLUTION

### A Self-Discovery workbook

### Rui M. Lima, MA, MSW, LICSW

**2017**

©

# DEDICATION

**This workbook is dedicated to the people who struggle with uncontrollable anger, to the people who found the understanding, determination, attitude and resolution to discover their inner strengths and find sublime self-control.**

# RUI M. LIMA, MA, MSW, LICSW

I decided to write this anger management workbook to simplify ways to deal with anger, cultivate prevention of anger outbursts, and increase self-understanding of manifestations of anger without disrupting the harmony of emotions.

We are the way we perceive and feel the universe. The way we use anger determines our capacity to organize our thoughts and live a troubled or peaceful life. We can self-discover the dynamics of our motivations and inner selves by recognizing the roots of our attitudes and behaviors, and by fostering the process of assertiveness, self-awareness, self-care, self-regulation, self-actualization, insight, hope, healing, and transformation.

You will challenge your belief system, overwhelming behaviors, and misunderstood feelings and thoughts, when completing this workbook. You will identify physical, emotional and cognitive cues that may trigger uncontrollable anger and master the application of mindfulness and self-control. You will realize that shame, guilt, frustration, disappointment, annoyance, irritation, resentment and other elements are contributors of anger. You will learn stress management, conflict resolution, decision making, problem solving, assertiveness and mindfulness coping skills, and demonstrate knowledge of application of coping skills with others, with your psychotherapist or in group. You will comprehend the underlying forces of healthy and unhealthy relationships, and improve your interpersonal relationships.

I have learned that personal awareness and growth leads to an increased sense of identity, personal power, creativity, and greater purpose. The goal of this workbook is to have you acknowledge your strengths through your own self-discovery from your childhood to the present time, and reveal fundamental components that will assist you in recognizing the true meaning of life. You will understand how environment and circumstances affect behaviors, and how powerful inner motivations make the person you became.

I hold a Masters of Arts degree in Rehabilitation Counseling from Assumption College, and a Master of Social Work degree from Bridgewater State University. I am a Licensed Independent Clinical Social Worker in the states of Massachusetts and Rhode Island. My experience as a psychotherapist includes the use of mindfulness and eclectic psychotherapy to address fluctuations in mood, substance abuse, addictions, and feelings of dissatisfaction with self, with relationships, and with work. I hope you discover how amazing life is without conflict.

# Table of Contents

**Photos by Patricia Almeida Lima**

**"Nothing goes away until has taught us what we need to know."**

**Buddha**

# INTRODUCTION TO ANGER MANAGEMENT WORKBOOK

## What is Anger?

Anger is a secondary reactive emotion to fear, displeasure, pain, provocation, irritation, frustration, resentment, jealousy, dislike, disagreement, threat, criticism, disappointment, loss, guilt, shame, annoyance, events, situations, people and things. Anger can empower, energize, change and motivate ourselves to achieve great purposes, but also can destroy everything that we had accomplished if it is not appropriately controlled.

Anger can be controlled by understanding its roots and perceived intentions. The way we perceive a situation, an event, a person, a place, a thing, what has been said or done, determines how we react when angry. It is our reaction that shows our self-control or lack of it. We must be in control of ourselves if we want to have a life free of conflict and embraced by mindfulness peace, resolution, and understanding.

We must increase awareness of past and present physical cues and emotional responses to anger, and strategically convince ourselves that the best response to anger must include self-control, self-awareness, and self-regulation.

**We become the thoughts that we act upon. Our behaviors may determine the level of consciousness of our physical and psychological fears and pains. We must ask ourselves what has been causing our pain and fear, and what we had done to conquer such fears and pains. We are what we feel, and our feelings may respond to physical and psychological illness through the avenues of short temperament and angry outbursts. We can and we will control our anger.**

- **How angry are you today? Please circle one.**

| 0 | 1 | 2 | 3 | 4 | 5 | 6 | 7 | 8 | 9 | 10 | + |
|---|---|---|---|---|---|---|---|---|---|---|---|
| None | | | | | | | | | | Extremely | |

Please explain your choice: ________________________________

________________________________

________________________________

- **How angry were you last week? Please circle one.**

| 0 | 1 | 2 | 3 | 4 | 5 | 6 | 7 | 8 | 9 | 10 | + |
|---|---|---|---|---|---|---|---|---|---|---|---|
| None | | | | | | | | | | Extremely | |

Please explain your choice: ________________________________

________________________________

________________________________

<h1 style="text-align:center">YOU</h1>

**People lose their health, their wealth, their family, relationships, their loved ones, their sense of self, their purpose in life, and even their lives due to rage or anger outbursts.**

**Please describe everything you know about yourself from birth until the current time and how anger interferes with your happiness. Include your interactions with childhood friends, family dynamics, school encounters, romantic relationships, work environment, legal and illegal activities, events that led to trouble with the law, and behaviors that resulted on chaotic lifestyle. Additionally, include other experiences and events that shaped the person you are today. Please write about who, when, where, why, and how you first experience anger. It is important to be honest in your comments, opinions, and observations. Your memory will assist you in understanding the birth of your anger.**

# SELF-DISCOVERY

**We grow healthy emotionally when we have complete self-awareness and understanding of our inner selves' strengths and life purposes. Self-control is gained by application of mindfulness knowledge and experience of the self.**

- **How much Self-control do you currently have? Please circle one.**

**0     1     2     3     4     5     6     7     8     9     10     +**
No
Self-control                                                              Extremely Self-Control

**Please explain your choice:** _______________________________________

_______________________________________________________________

_______________________________________________________________

- **How much did you loss because of your anger? Please circle one.**

**0     1     2     3     4     5     6     7     8     9     10     +**
Lost
Nothing                                                                         Lost a lot

**Please explain your choice:** _______________________________________

_______________________________________________________________

_______________________________________________________________

- **How much do you love and care about yourself? Please circle one.**

**0     1     2     3     4     5     6     7     8     9     10     +**
Do not
Love or Care                                                           Extremely Love & Care

**Please explain your choice:** _______________________________________

_______________________________________________________________

- **How much do you dislike people? Please circle one.**

**0     1     2     3     4     5     6     7     8     9     10     +**
I like
people                                                                      Extremely dislike

**Please explain your choice:** _______________________________________

_______________________________________________________________

We must self-motivate, love and care about ourselves, and apply what is known as beneficial to our inner selves. We must learn, participate, understand and enrich the following:

- **Self-understanding**          **(needs, purposes, goals, objectives)**
- **Self-care**          **(body, mind, emotionally, spirituality)**
- **Self-awareness**          **(past and present)**
- **Self-direction**          **(motivation, beneficial way)**
- **Self- commitment**          **(contract, promise)**
- **Self-change**          **(courage, determination, ownership)**
- **Self- responsibility**          **(fairness, justice, morality, integrity)**
- **Self-love**          **(unconditionally)**
- **Self-accountability**          **(fearlessness, honesty)**
- **Self-flexibility**          **(workable; dependable)**
- **Self-insight**          **(visionary, awake)**
- **Self-discovery**          **(finding, hope)**
- **Self-motivation**          **(genuine enthusiasm)**
- **Self-discipline**          **(control, happiness)**
- **Self-empowerment**          **(inner force, energy)**
- **Self-esteem**          **(capability, belief)**
- **Self-reliance**          **(confidence, thrust)**
- **Self-acceptance**          **(awareness of strength, happiness)**
- **Self-worth**          **(value, respect)**
- **Self-realization**          (________________________________)
- **Self-healing**          (________________________________)
- **Self-actualization**          (________________________________)
- **Self-regulation**          (________________________________)
- **Self-control**          (________________________________)

**Sometimes the demands of repetition, failure, chaotic lifestyle, painful experiences, careless thoughts, abusive relationships, and impulsive risky behaviors, lead us to change and learn healthy coping skills, including anger management. We must hold on to self-acceptance, self-responsibility, self-accountability, and self-discipline, in order to prevent, understand and find resolution to our anger.**

- **How motivated are you to learn anger management coping skills? Please circle one.**

| **0** | **1** | **2** | **3** | **4** | **5** | **6** | **7** | **8** | **9** | **10** | **+** |
|---|---|---|---|---|---|---|---|---|---|---|---|
| **Not motivated** | | | | | | | | | | **Very motivated** | |

**Please explain your choice:** _______________________________________

_____________________________________________________________

# Be the positive energy that connects you to the universe

In order to remain free of self-destructive thoughts and behaviors, we must discover ourselves and acquire full knowledge about ourselves. We must seek our guiding manual and master our desires. We must understand the roots of our suffering and identify our strengths. We must comprehend, believe, and integrate into our sense of being human, the greater purpose of our lives, without anger outbursts or destructive behaviors.

**Please check what it is important to you:**

| Item | √ | Item | √ | Item | √ | Item | √ | Item | √ |
|---|---|---|---|---|---|---|---|---|---|
| Relationships | | Strength | | Culture | | Honesty | | Creativity | |
| Universe | | Inner self | | Reason | | Fitness | | Media | |
| Intimacy | | Data | | Introvert | | Health | | Travel | |
| Leisure | | Nature | | Shy | | Appearance | | Drugs | |
| Independence | | Education | | Trustworthy | | Control | | Virtue | |
| Money | | Young-self | | Acceptance | | Religion | | Image | |
| Art | | Input | | Love | | Joy | | Sexuality | |
| Internet | | Socialize | | Impossible | | Risk | | Exercise | |
| Space | | Mother | | Sincere | | Fun | | Training | |
| Awareness | | Yearns | | Mystical | | Play | | Motivation | |
| Growth | | Life | | Able | | Humor | | Flexibility | |
| Rigidity | | Openness | | Real | | Family | | Transportation | |
| Energy | | Values | | Violence | | Friends | | Shelter | |
| Acceptance | | Ethics | | Experience | | Obligations | | Food | |
| Talents | | Theories | | Lucrative | | Work | | Hobbies | |
| Morals | | Occult | | Office | | Sex | | Time | |
| Assurance | | Oxygen | | Uniqueness | | Race | | Faith | |
| Needs | | Trust | | Sun glasses | | Gender | | Self-control | |
| Time | | Skills | | Today | | Things | | Alcohol | |
| People | | Softness | | Ambition | | Places | | Clothing | |
| Nothing | | Alone | | Goals | | Death | | Tomorrow | |

| Item | √ | Please add | √ |
|---|---|---|---|
| Responsibility | | Other:___________________ | |
| Accountability | | Other:___________________ | |
| Self-determination | | Other:___________________ | |
| Self-actualization | | Other:___________________ | |
| School | | Other:___________________ | |
| Self-regulation | | Other:___________________ | |
| Self-esteem | | Other:___________________ | |
| Articulateness | | Other:___________________ | |
| Self-control | | ___________________ | |

**WHO ARE YOU?**

Name: ________________________________________ Age: ______________

Gender: ______________ Birth Date: ________________SSN: ______________

Height: ______________ Weight: __________

Who give you your name? ________________________________________

What is the meaning of your name? ________________________________________

- **How much do you know yourself? Please circle one.**

| 0 | 1 | 2 | 3 | 4 | 5 | 6 | 7 | 8 | 9 | 10 | + |
|---|---|---|---|---|---|---|---|---|---|----|---|

**0**
Do not

**10** **+**
Extremely

Please explain your choice: ________________________________________

________________________________________

### Ethnic Group:

1. African American/ Black____    2.Azorean____    4. French____ 5.German____

6. Hispanic / Latino____    7.Italian____    8.Irish ____ 9. Native American____

10. Portuguese____    11. Other: ________________________________

### Race:

1. American Indian/ Native American____ 2. African American/ Black____    3.Asian____

3. White Caucasian____    4.Bi-Racial: ________________________________

5. Other: ________________________________________

### Sexual Orientation:

( ) Heterosexual ( ) Bisexual ( ) Homosexual ( ) Transgender  ( ) pan-sexual

( ) Other: ________________________________

A)  What are your Strengths?

_______________________________________________________
_______________________________________________________
_______________________________________________________
_______________________________________________________
_______________________________________________________
_______________________________________________________
_______________________________________________________

B)  What are your Abilities and Skills? (e.g. vocational)

_______________________________________________________
_______________________________________________________
_______________________________________________________
_______________________________________________________
_______________________________________________________
_______________________________________________________
_______________________________________________________

C)  What are your Needs?

_______________________________________________________
_______________________________________________________
_______________________________________________________
_______________________________________________________
_______________________________________________________
_______________________________________________________
_______________________________________________________
_______________________________________________________

D) What are your Goals? (What would you like to accomplish in one month; three months, six months, one year, two years, and five years).

________________________________________________

________________________________________________

________________________________________________

________________________________________________

________________________________________________

________________________________________________

________________________________________________

________________________________________________

________________________________________________

________________________________________________

E) What are the favorite things you like to do in your free time and with whom? (e.g. hobbies, sports, family involvement, etc.).

________________________________________________

________________________________________________

________________________________________________

________________________________________________

F) Please write everything you would like to change in your life.

________________________________________________

________________________________________________

________________________________________________

________________________________________________

________________________________________________

________________________________________________

G) Please describe all your achievements?

_______________________________________________________

_______________________________________________________

_______________________________________________________

_______________________________________________________

_______________________________________________________

_______________________________________________________

_______________________________________________________

H) Please write everything you have lost due to your anger.

_______________________________________________________

_______________________________________________________

_______________________________________________________

_______________________________________________________

_______________________________________________________

_______________________________________________________

_______________________________________________________

_______________________________________________________

_______________________________________________________

_______________________________________________________

_______________________________________________________

_______________________________________________________

_______________________________________________________

_______________________________________________________

_______________________________________________________

_______________________________________________________

_______________________________________________________

<u>**ENVIRONMENT**</u>

1. Where do you live?

City: _______________________________ State:_____________ Zip: __________

<u>**Household / Living Arrangements:**</u>

1. House/Apartment__ 2. Group Home__ 3. Room/Boarding house__ 4. Shelter__

5. Other: _________________________________________________________________

1. How many times have you moved in the last year? _______________

2. Do you feel you live in a safe place? YES/NO (Please circle one)

Please explain:

_________________________________________________________________

_________________________________________________________________

_________________________________________________________________

_________________________________________________________________

3. Who lives with you?

_________________________________________________________________

_________________________________________________________________

_________________________________________________________________

_________________________________________________________________

4. In the past year, has your partner, family member, or stranger pushed you, punched you, kicked you, hit you, or threatened to hurt you? YES/NO (Please circle one)

If yes, who: _____________________ When: _______________________________

Why: _____________________________________________________________

_________________________________________________________________

_________________________________________________________________

_________________________________________________________________

( ) Never married ( ) Single ( ) Married ( ) Separated ( ) Divorced ( ) Widowed

1.  How many children do you have? _______ With how many partners: ________

2.  What are their ages and gender? _________________________________________

3.  Where do your children live now?

________________________________________________________________________

________________________________________________________________________

4.  Who takes care of your children?

________________________________________________________________________

________________________________________________________________________

________________________________________________________________________

5.  Did you neglect your children due to legal problems? YES/NO. Please explain.

________________________________________________________________________

________________________________________________________________________

________________________________________________________________________

6.  Are you currently in a romantic relationship? YES/NO ( Please circle one)

Please explain: _________________________________________________________

________________________________________________________________________

7.  Does your partner uses or used drugs? YES/NO (Please circle one)

Please explain: _________________________________________________________

________________________________________________________________________

8.  Does your partner have or had anger issues? YES/NO (Please circle one)

Please explain: _________________________________________________________

________________________________________________________________________

9.  How long have you been with your partner?

________________________________________________________________________

**10.** What do you do for fun with your partner?

_______________________________________________________

_______________________________________________________

_______________________________________________________

**11.** How did you meet your current partner?

_______________________________________________________

_______________________________________________________

_______________________________________________________

**12.** What have you learnt with your partner?

_______________________________________________________

_______________________________________________________

_______________________________________________________

**13.** How many friends do you have? _______________________

**14.** How many acquaintances you have? ____________________

**15.** How many friends do you have who are currently sober and in recovery? ___________

**16.** How many friends do you have who are currently using illegal drugs? ____________

**17.**  How many friends do you have who had overdosed in drugs? ____________________

**18.** How many of your friends do have a job? ______________________________

**19.** How many of your friends use cannabis? ________________________________

**20.** How many of your friends drink alcohol? ________________________________

**21.** How many of your friends attend AA/NA self-help groups? _________________

**22.** How many of your friends have been in prison? ___________________________

**23.** How many of your friends are violent? __________________________________

**24.** How many of your friends have unhealthy relationship? ___________________

**25.** How many of your friends have anger issues? _____________________________

**26.** How many of your friends have been victims of abuse? _____________________

**27.** How many of your friends are abusers? _________________________________

**28.** How do you describe your friends?

_______________________________________________________________

_______________________________________________________________

_______________________________________________________________

_______________________________________________________________

**29.** What did you learn with your friends and family members? Please elaborate the good, the bad, and the ugly that you have experienced and learned from your friends and family members.

_______________________________________________________________

_______________________________________________________________

_______________________________________________________________

_______________________________________________________________

_______________________________________________________________

_______________________________________________________________

_______________________________________________________________

_______________________________________________________________

_______________________________________________________________

_______________________________________________________________

_______________________________________________________________

_______________________________________________________________

**21.** Were you popular in school or in your neighborhood? YES/NO (Please circle one) Please elaborate.

_______________________________________________________________

_______________________________________________________________

_______________________________________________________________

_______________________________________________________________

## WHEN YOU WERE A CHILD

1.  Did either parent have a drug or alcohol problem? YES/NO (Please circle one)
If yes, who? How long was the problem? What do you remember about the problem?
How has this problem affected your life as a child and now as an adult?

_______________________________________________________________________

_______________________________________________________________________

_______________________________________________________________________

_______________________________________________________________________

_______________________________________________________________________

_______________________________________________________________________

_______________________________________________________________________

2.  Were you exposed to domestic violence growing up? YES/NO (Please circle one)
If yes, what do you remember about it? How do you think violence affected your life
as a child and now as an adult?

_______________________________________________________________________

_______________________________________________________________________

_______________________________________________________________________

_______________________________________________________________________

_______________________________________________________________________

_______________________________________________________________________

_______________________________________________________________________

3.  Were you raised in part or all of the time by foster parents or relatives? (Other
than your parents) YES/NO. Please explain.

_______________________________________________________________________

_______________________________________________________________________

_______________________________________________________________________

_______________________________________________________________________

4.  How often did your parents/guardians ground you or put you in time out?  Please
elaborate
( ) Frequently   ( ) Often   ( ) Occasionally   ( ) Rarely   ( ) Never

_______________________________________________________________________

_______________________________________________________________________

Please explain

5. Do you feel you were physically abused      YES/NO

_______________________________________________

_______________________________________________

_______________________________________________

6. Do you feel you were neglected?      YES/NO

_______________________________________________

_______________________________________________

_______________________________________________

7. Do you feel you were hurt in a sexual way?      YES/NO

_______________________________________________

_______________________________________________

_______________________________________________

8. Did your parents ever hurt you when they were out of control?      YES/NO

_______________________________________________

_______________________________________________

_______________________________________________

### EARLY FAMILY

1. Did you live in a two-parent family? YES/NO. If yes until when?

_______________________________________________

_______________________________________________

_______________________________________________

If no, why not? _______________________________________________

_______________________________________________

_______________________________________________

_______________________________________________

2. Do you have siblings? YES/NO. If yes, how many? _______________________

    Did they live in the same family? YES/NO.  If no, why not?

    _______________________________________________________________________

    _______________________________________________________________________

    _______________________________________________________________________

3. Do you get along with your siblings? YES/NO. Please elaborate.

    _______________________________________________________________________

    _______________________________________________________________________

4. Did your family have ongoing family difficulties? YES/NO. If yes, please
   explain.

    _______________________________________________________________________

    _______________________________________________________________________

    _______________________________________________________________________

5. Did you like school? YES/NO. If yes, please explain.

    _______________________________________________________________________

    _______________________________________________________________________

6. Did you have difficulties at school? YES/NO. If yes, please explain.

    _______________________________________________________________________

    _______________________________________________________________________

    _______________________________________________________________________

7. Did you have behavior problems at school? YES/NO. If yes, please explain.

    _______________________________________________________________________

    _______________________________________________________________________

    _______________________________________________________________________

8. Were you bullied at school? YES/NO. If yes, please explain.

    _______________________________________________________________________

    _______________________________________________________________________

    _______________________________________________________________________

9. How many fights did you have with your peers at school? _______________
   Please explain

    _______________________________________________________________________

    _______________________________________________________________________

    _______________________________________________________________________

# CURRENT FAMILY PROFILE

1.  Who lives with you?

_____________________________________________________________

_____________________________________________________________

_____________________________________________________________

2.  How do you describe your relationship with your parents?

_____________________________________________________________

_____________________________________________________________

_____________________________________________________________

3.  How do you describe your relationship with your partner?

_____________________________________________________________

_____________________________________________________________

_____________________________________________________________

_____________________________________________________________

4.  How do you describe your relationship with your sibling(s)?

_____________________________________________________________

_____________________________________________________________

_____________________________________________________________

_____________________________________________________________

5.  How do you describe your relationship with your children?

_____________________________________________________________

_____________________________________________________________

_____________________________________________________________

_____________________________________________________________

6.  With whom do you talk about your problems?

_____________________________________________________________

_____________________________________________________________

7.  Do you feel that you have a healthy support system? YES/NO. If yes, please explain

_____________________________________________________________

_____________________________________________________________

_____________________________________________________________

**EDUCATION**

1.  How many years of school have you completed? ___________

    ( ) High school Diploma ( ) Some College ( ) College degree ( ) Other

2.  What is the name of the last school you attended? ___________________

3.  Would you like to return to school? YES/NO. Please explain.

    _______________________________________________________________

    _______________________________________________________________

4.  What did you like about school? Please explain.

    _______________________________________________________________

    _______________________________________________________________

    _______________________________________________________________

5.  What did you dislike about school? Please explain.

    _______________________________________________________________

    _______________________________________________________________

    _______________________________________________________________

6.  Did you complete any certification programs? YES/NO. Please explain.

    _______________________________________________________________

    _______________________________________________________________

    _______________________________________________________________

**EMPLOYMENT**

1.  Are you employed? YES/NO. If YES, how long have you been employed?

    _______________________________________________________________

2.  What type of employment is it?

    _______________________________________________________________

3.  Where do you get your financial support?

    _______________________________________________________________

4.  Were you in the military? YES/NO. If YES, please explain.

    _______________________________________________________________

## LEISURE TIME ACTIVITY

1.  What are the favorite things you do during your free time? With whom?

_______________________________________________________________

_______________________________________________________________

_______________________________________________________________

_______________________________________________________________

_______________________________________________________________

2.  What activities are you involved within the community?

_______________________________________________________________

_______________________________________________________________

_______________________________________________________________

3.  What would you like to do to have fun?

_______________________________________________________________

_______________________________________________________________

_______________________________________________________________

_______________________________________________________________

_______________________________________________________________

_______________________________________________________________

## SPIRITUAL LIFE/CHURCH MEMBERSHIP

1.  How strong are your family's religious beliefs or practices?
    ( ) Very Strong   ( ) Moderate strong  ( ) Not strong   ( ) No religious

    What religion/Church/temple do you attend?

_______________________________________________________________

_______________________________________________________________

_______________________________________________________________

2.  Is spirituality important in your life? YES/NO. Please explain.

_______________________________________________________________

_______________________________________________________________

_______________________________________________________________

**FAMILY HISTORY**

1.  Has any member of your family been treated for PSYCHIATRIC problems?
    YES/NO. If yes, who?

    ___________________________________________________________

    ___________________________________________________________

    ___________________________________________________________

2.  Has any member of your family been treated for MEDICAL problems? YES/NO.
    If yes, who?

    ___________________________________________________________

    ___________________________________________________________

    ___________________________________________________________

3.  Has any member of your family been treated for SUBSTANCE ABUSE
    problems? YES/NO. If yes, who?

    ___________________________________________________________

    ___________________________________________________________

4.  Has any member of your family been involved with the legal system? YES/NO. If
    yes, who?

    ___________________________________________________________

    ___________________________________________________________

    ___________________________________________________________

5.  Has any member of your family been involved with domestic violence or ANGER
    MANAGEMENT programs? YES/NO. If yes, who?

    ___________________________________________________________

    ___________________________________________________________

    ___________________________________________________________

**FAMILY ACTIVITIES**

1. What does your family do together for fun?

    ___________________________________________________________

    ___________________________________________________________

    ___________________________________________________________

## ANGER, ALCOHOL, DRUGS AND JAIL

1. How many times have you been in trouble due to your anger? _______________
2. How many times did you use alcohol or drugs because of your anger? _______
3. Do you have a drug of choice? _____________________________________________
4. How many detoxes have you attended? ______________________________________
5. How many times have you overdosed? _______________________________________
6. How many times have you had a relapse? ____________________________________
7. How long ago was your longest sobriety time? _________ and when? _______
8. How many times have you tried to cut down on drugs and/or alcohol? _______
9. How many times have you attended self-help groups last week? ___________
10. How many times have you been on probation? ________________________________
11. How many times have you been on parole? ___________________________________
12. How many times you had served a sentence or been incarcerated? _________
13. How many times have you been arrested? ____________________________________
14. How many sober houses programs have you attended? _________________________
15. How many half-way houses programs have you attended? ______________________
16. Have you attended any of these programs?
    ( ) Anger management
    ( ) Domestic violence
    ( ) Parenting
    ( ) Substance Abuse Program: ___________________________________________
    ( ) Mental Health Program: _____________________________________________
    ( ) Other: ______________________________________________________________

Please explain when and where you completed programs:

_______________________________________________________________________________

_______________________________________________________________________________

_______________________________________________________________________________

**17. How tired are you of doing the same things, falling for the same or similar problems and expecting different results?**

**Please circle one.**

| 0 | 1 | 2 | 3 | 4 | 5 | 6 | 7 | 8 | 9 | 10 |
|---|---|---|---|---|---|---|---|---|---|---|
| Not Tired | | | | | | | | | | Very Tired |

**Please explain:** ___________________________________________________________

_______________________________________________________________________________

_______________________________________________________________________________

_______________________________________________________________________________

# HELP AND SUPPORT

1. Who can you count on to be dependable when you need help? (Write their initials and their relationship to you).

a) ____________________  b) ____________________  c) ____________

d) ____________________  e) ____________________  f) ____________

( ) If no one, explain.

_______________________________________________________________

_______________________________________________________________

2. How satisfied are you with their support?
( ) Very satisfied   ( ) Satisfied   ( ) Very dissatisfied   ( ) Dissatisfied
( ) No support

3. Who do you feel loves you deeply? (Please write their initials and their relationship to you).

a) ____________________  b) ____________________  c) ____________

( ) If no one, explain. _______________________________________

4. Are you currently involved or receiving services from the following?

( ) Department of Children and Family: ____________________
( ) Probation: ____________________________________________
( ) Parole: _______________________________________________
( ) Department of Mental Health: __________________________
( ) Rehabilitation Services: ______________________________
( ) Court: ________________________________________________
( ) Community Resources: __________________________________
( ) Other: ________________________________________________
( ) Other: ________________________________________________

5. Do you have an AA/NA sponsor? __________________________________
6. Do you have a pet? ____________________________________________
7. Do you trust anybody? _________________________________________
8. Do you pray? __________________________________________________
9. Do you talk to family members? _______________________________
10. Do you enjoy friendships? ____________________________________
11. Do you feel safe when in the company of close friends? Please explain.

_______________________________________________________________

_______________________________________________________________

_______________________________________________________________

# MENTAL HEALTH AND SUBSTANCE ABUSE DISORDERS

1. Have you been diagnosed with a mental health disorder and a substance abuse disorder? YES/NO. Please explain.

__________________________________________________________________

__________________________________________________________________

__________________________________________________________________

2. Do you take medication due to a mental health disorder? YES/NO. Please explain.

__________________________________________________________________

__________________________________________________________________

__________________________________________________________________

3. Did you use to take medication due to a mental health disorder? YES/NO. Please explain.

__________________________________________________________________

__________________________________________________________________

__________________________________________________________________

4. Do you take medication due to a substance abuse disorder? YES/NO. Please explain.

__________________________________________________________________

__________________________________________________________________

__________________________________________________________________

5. Does medication help you with your mental health disorder? YES/NO. Please explain.

__________________________________________________________________

__________________________________________________________________

__________________________________________________________________

6. Do you agree about taking medication for a mental health disorder? YES/NO. Please explain.

__________________________________________________________________

__________________________________________________________________

7.  Do you agree to take medication for a substance abuse disorder? YES/NO. Please explain.

_____________________________________________________________

_____________________________________________________________

_____________________________________________________________

_____________________________________________________________

8.  How long have you been involved with psychiatric services? Please explain

_____________________________________________________________

_____________________________________________________________

_____________________________________________________________

_____________________________________________________________

9.  In your opinion, what are the pros and cons of taking medications?

_____________________________________________________________

_____________________________________________________________

_____________________________________________________________

_____________________________________________________________

10.  Do you have family members who take medication due to mental illness and/or substance abuse issues? YES/NO. Please explain.

_____________________________________________________________

_____________________________________________________________

_____________________________________________________________

_____________________________________________________________

11. Have you been diagnosed with any of the following? √ if yes, when?

    **a)**  ( )Anxiety :_________________________________________

    **b)**  ( )Depression: ______________________________________

    **c)**  ( )Mood disorder:___________________________________

    **d)**  ( )PTSD: __________________________________________

    **e)**  ( ) Borderline: _____________________________________

    **f)**  ( )Anti-social:______________________________________

    **g)**  ( )Avoidance: ______________________________________

    **h)**  ( ) Schizophrenia: __________________________________

    **i)**  ( ) Other: _________________________________________

_____________________________________________________________

**What are the most important aspects about yourself that you were able to identify by answering the previous questions?**

# WORDS ABOUT FEELINGS

When we feel, we liberate life to its most beautiful human form. Feelings connect us to each other and to the universe. We are able to feel when we allow ourselves to receive the full magic and energy from life. Feelings are not good or bad, they are the amplitude of our needs. We can deeply engage in the process of self-discovery when we clarify our awareness and understanding about why we feel a certain way.

How do you feel today? √

| √ | | √ | | √ | | √ | |
|---|---|---|---|---|---|---|---|
| Awe | Aggravated | Caring | Blessed | Relieved | |
| Delighted | Disgruntled | Stimulated | Courageous | Inspired | |
| Playful | Adventurous | Yearning | Disturbed | Tender | |
| Calm | Contempt | Empathy | Grateful | Angry | |
| Centered | Cynical | Fascinated | Guilt | Miserable | |
| Thrusting | Valiant | Useless | Helpless | Overwhelmed | |
| Excited | Furious | Discouraged | Hesitant | Perplexed | |
| Accepting | Afraid | Appreciative | Humbled | Dread | |
| Enthusiastic | Frustrated | Disappointed | Impotent | Puzzled | |
| Engaged | Irritated | Anxious | Incapable | Detached | |
| Eager | Disturbed | Anguish | Joy | Helpful | |
| Relaxed | Daring | Indifferent | Nervous | Passive | |
| Renewed | Determined | Isolated | Panic | Aggressive | |
| Free | Grouchy | Grief | Perplexed | Troubled | |
| Ecstatic | Edgy | Depressed | Powerless | Curious | |
| Fulfilled | Hostile | Heartbroken | Questioning | Withdrawn | |
| Happy | Impatient | Hopeless | Rejecting | Uncomfortable | |
| Invigorated | Irate | Lonely | Reluctant | Embarrassed | |
| Rejuvenated | Confident | Distant | Remorseful | Intense | |
| Content | Disdain | Intrigued | Sad | Jealous | |
| Vibrant | Warm | Lucky | Safe | Detached | |
| Satisfied | Proud | Resistant | Scared | Insecure | |
| Radiant | Brave | Aloof | Self-loving | Open | |
| Amazed | Agitated | Affectionate | Sensitive | Peaceful | |
| Lively | Moody | Longing | Shocked | Zestful | |
| Mindful | Outraged | Melancholy | Skeptical | Mischievous | |
| Refreshed | Capable | Bored | Sorry | Alert | |
| Motivated | Resentful | Sorrow | Suspicious | Goofy | |
| Serene | Strong | Uneasy | Terrified | Distant | |
| Bliss | Bitter | Compassion | Thankful | Tranquil | |
| Patient | Upset | Unhappy | Ungrounded | Amorous | |
| Peaceful | Vindictive | Weary | Unsure | Friendly | |
| Thrilled | Worthy | Ashamed | Worried | Distracted | |
| Concerned | Annoyed | Surprised | Proud | Loved | |

# ANGER, FEELINGS AND THOUGHTS

1. What were the feelings and thoughts that you had **BEFORE** your last anger outburst? Please explain.

_______________________________________________________________________

_______________________________________________________________________

_______________________________________________________________________

2. What were the feelings and thoughts that you had **AFTER** your last anger outburst? Please explain.

_______________________________________________________________________

_______________________________________________________________________

_______________________________________________________________________

**3.** What were the feelings and thoughts that you were unable to control and understand **BEFORE** your last anger outburst? Please explain.

_______________________________________________________________________

_______________________________________________________________________

_______________________________________________________________________

4. What were the feelings and thoughts that you were unable to control and understand **AFTER** your anger outburst? Please explain.

_______________________________________________________________________

_______________________________________________________________________

_______________________________________________________________________

5. What were the feelings and thoughts that made you accept that you have problems due to uncontrollable anger? Please explain.

_______________________________________________________________________

_______________________________________________________________________

_______________________________________________________________________

# ANGER, BEHAVIORS AND ATTITUDES

1.  What **ARE** the behaviors and attitudes that **CURRENTLY** hurt you physically? Please explain.

_______________________________________________________________

_______________________________________________________________

_______________________________________________________________

2.  What **ARE** the behaviors and attitudes that **CURRENTLY** hurt you emotionally? Please explain.

_______________________________________________________________

_______________________________________________________________

_______________________________________________________________

3. What **ARE** the behaviors and attitudes that **CURRENTLY** hurt your relationships? Please explain.

_______________________________________________________________

_______________________________________________________________

_______________________________________________________________

4. What **ARE** the behaviors and attitudes that **CURRENTLY** affect your work performance? Please explain.

_______________________________________________________________

_______________________________________________________________

_______________________________________________________________

5. What **ARE** the behaviors and attitudes that you are **CURRENTLY** unable to control? Please explain.

_______________________________________________________________

_______________________________________________________________

_______________________________________________________________

_______________________________________________________________

6. What **ARE** the obsessive-compulsive behaviors that you **CURRENTLY** have? Please explain.

_______________________________________________

_______________________________________________

_______________________________________________

_______________________________________________

7. What **WERE** the behaviors and attitudes that hurt you physically when expressing anger? Please explain.

_______________________________________________

_______________________________________________

_______________________________________________

_______________________________________________

8. What **WERE** the behaviors and attitudes that hurt you emotionally when expressing anger? Please explain.

_______________________________________________

_______________________________________________

_______________________________________________

_______________________________________________

9. What **WERE** the behaviors and attitudes that hurt your relationships when expressing anger? Please explain.

_______________________________________________

_______________________________________________

_______________________________________________

_______________________________________________

10. What **WERE** the behaviors and attitudes that affected your work performance when expressing anger? Please explain.

_______________________________________________

_______________________________________________

_______________________________________________

_______________________________________________

_______________________________________________

_______________________________________________

# I AM

Who are you? Please complete the following:

I am _______________________________________________.

I am _______________________________________________.

I am _______________________________________________.

I am _______________________________________________.

I am _______________________________________________.

I am _______________________________________________.

I am _______________________________________________.

I am _______________________________________________.

I am _______________________________________________.

I am _______________________________________________.

I am _______________________________________________.

I am _______________________________________________.

I am _______________________________________________.

I am _______________________________________________.

I am _______________________________________________.

I am _______________________________________________.

I am _______________________________________________.

I am _______________________________________________.

I am _______________________________________________.

I am _______________________________________________.

I am _______________________________________________.

I am _______________________________________________.

I am _______________________________________________.

I am _______________________________________________.

I am _______________________________________________.

I am _______________________________________________.

I am _______________________________________________.

I am _______________________________________________.

Think about your emotions, attitudes and behaviors when you are angry, and complete the following:

**When I am angry I** _______________________________________________ .

**When I am angry I** _______________________________________________ .

**When I am angry I** _______________________________________________ .

**When I am angry I** _______________________________________________ .

**When I am angry I** _______________________________________________ .

**When I am angry I** _______________________________________________ .

**When I am angry I** _______________________________________________ .

**When I am angry I** _______________________________________________ .

**When I am angry I** _______________________________________________ .

**When I am angry I** _______________________________________________ .

**When I am angry I** _______________________________________________ .

**When I am angry I** _______________________________________________ .

**When I am angry I** _______________________________________________ .

**When I am angry I** _______________________________________________ .

**When I am angry I** _______________________________________________ .

**When I am angry I** _______________________________________________ .

**When I am angry I** _______________________________________________ .

**When I am angry I** _______________________________________________ .

**When I am angry I** _______________________________________________ .

**When I am angry I** _______________________________________________ .

**When I am angry I** _______________________________________________ .

**When I am angry I** _______________________________________________ .

**When I am angry I** _______________________________________________ .

**When I am angry I** _______________________________________________ .

**When I am angry I** _______________________________________________ .

**When I am angry I** _______________________________________________ .

# ASSERTIVENESS

**Assertive people are able to communicate their thoughts, needs, and feelings without offending others. They respect others rights and their own rights, and do not deny the right of others. Passive people tend to the needs of others before their own needs. Aggressive people definitely believe in their own rights but do not believe others have rights too.**

1.  What style do you use when interacting with people?
    The assertive style______
    The passive style________
    The aggressive style______

    Please explain your choice: _______________________________________________

    _______________________________________________________________________

    _______________________________________________________________________

    _______________________________________________________________________

2.  Are you happy with the decisions you make? YES/NO Please explain.

    _______________________________________________________________________

    _______________________________________________________________________

    _______________________________________________________________________

3.  Do you think your needs are overlooked? YES/NO Please explain.

    _______________________________________________________________________

    _______________________________________________________________________

    _______________________________________________________________________

4.  Do you think you deserve more respect? YES/NO Please explain.

    _______________________________________________________________________

    _______________________________________________________________________

    _______________________________________________________________________

5.  Do you think you cooperate with others in a fair and consistent way? YES/NO
    Please explain.

    _______________________________________________________________________

    _______________________________________________________________________

    _______________________________________________________________________

6.  **My communication skills are**_____________________________________.

<pre>
0     1     2     3     4     5     6     7     8     9     10      +
Poor                                                          Excellent
</pre>

Please explain.

_______________________________________________________________

_______________________________________________________________

_______________________________________________________________

7.  Do you think you have the need to compete or prove yourself to others? YES/NO
    Please explain.

_______________________________________________________________

_______________________________________________________________

_______________________________________________________________

8.  Do you have difficulty keeping affectionate / romantic relationships? YES/NO
    Please explain.

_______________________________________________________________

_______________________________________________________________

_______________________________________________________________

9.  Do you assess situations and decide what action or behavior is most appropriate?
    YES/NO Please explain.

_______________________________________________________________

_______________________________________________________________

_______________________________________________________________

**Please reflect about your answers and read the characteristics of each style.**

| ASSERTIVENESS | PASSIVE | AGGRESSIVE |
| --- | --- | --- |
| Communicates well | Puts the needs of others first | Inappropriate behaviors |
| Appropriate behavior | Difficulty making decisions | Offensive and disrespectful |
| Respects others rights | Their needs are overlooked | Difficulty with relationships |
| Has self-control | Has low self-esteem | Poor communication skills |
| Direct and honest | May suffer from depression | Need to compete and prove |
| Polite and firm | May feel inferior to others | May have rude manners |
| Cooperative | Low self-respect | Hurtful and insulting |

We must be assertive in order to increase control of our lives. We must be clear about what we want, fair, consistent, honest, confident, flexible and able to compromise.

**Apply these simple rules**:

- Do not apologize or explain if you don't have to
- Use eye contact and calm voice
- Wait for your turn to speak
- Be clear, honest, and direct
- Recognize others rights and compromise if necessary or possible
- Don't except to convince
- Accept that life is not fair
- Be flexible and accept consequences
- Do not make excuses
- Pause and decide before replying
- Be aware of your body posture
- Be mindfulness of your surroundings
- Use I statements when necessary
- Do not be afraid to say No
- Be humble and firm
- Apply positive attitude
- Be knowledgeable about the subject of conversation
- Think before you open your mouth
- Select timing for conversations and environment
- Pay attention to details
- Value relationships and understand others stressors
- Validate others perceptions, valuable observations, and comments
- Agree and disagree without yelling or with an aggressive posture
- Ask for clarification when necessary
- Listen and focus what is actually being said
- Remain focus on the subject of discussion
- Acknowledge when you are wrong and apologize
- Select the level of your assertiveness with situation and person
- Positively practice what you had learned
- Always show respect and self-control
- Be polite and cooperate
- Understand others perceptions and attributes
- _______________________________________________
- _______________________________________________
- _______________________________________________
- _______________________________________________
- _______________________________________________

# I WANT TO HAVE...

Think about what you **WANT TO HAVE**. Please complete the following:

**I want to have**_______________________________________________________.

**I want to have**_______________________________________________________.

**I want to have**_______________________________________________________.

**I want to have**_______________________________________________________.

**I want to have**_______________________________________________________.

**I want to have**_______________________________________________________.

**I want to have**_______________________________________________________.

**I want to have**_______________________________________________________.

**I want to have**_______________________________________________________.

**I want to have**_______________________________________________________.

**I want to have**_______________________________________________________.

**I want to have**_______________________________________________________.

**I want to have**_______________________________________________________.

**I want to have**_______________________________________________________.

**I want to have**_______________________________________________________.

**I want to have**_______________________________________________________.

**I want to have**_______________________________________________________.

**I want to have**_______________________________________________________.

**I want to have**_______________________________________________________.

**I want to have**_______________________________________________________.

**I want to have**_______________________________________________________.

**I want to have**_______________________________________________________.

**I want to have**_______________________________________________________.

**I want to have**_______________________________________________________.

**I want to have**_______________________________________________________.

# I NEED TO DO…IN ORDER TO HAVE….

Please complete the following:

I need to do _______________________ in order to have_______________________.

I need to do _______________________ in order to have_______________________.

I need to do _______________________ in order to have_______________________.

I need to do _______________________ in order to have_______________________.

I need to do _______________________ in order to have_______________________.

I need to do _______________________ in order to have_______________________.

I need to do _______________________ in order to have_______________________.

I need to do _______________________ in order to have_______________________.

I need to do _______________________ in order to have_______________________.

I need to do _______________________ in order to have_______________________.

I need to do _______________________ in order to have_______________________.

I need to do _______________________ in order to have_______________________.

I need to do _______________________ in order to have_______________________.

I need to do _______________________ in order to have_______________________.

I need to do _______________________ in order to have_______________________.

I need to do _______________________ in order to have_______________________.

I need to do _______________________ in order to have_______________________.

I need to do _______________________ in order to have_______________________.

I need to do _______________________ in order to have_______________________.

I need to do _______________________ in order to have_______________________.

# I NEED...

Think about what you really **NEED** in your life.

Please complete the following:

**I need** _______________________________________.

**I need** _______________________________________.

**I need** _______________________________________.

**I need** _______________________________________.

**I need** _______________________________________.

**I need** _______________________________________.

**I need** _______________________________________.

**I need** _______________________________________.

**I need** _______________________________________.

**I need** _______________________________________.

**I need** _______________________________________.

**I need** _______________________________________.

**I need** _______________________________________.

**I need** _______________________________________.

**I need** _______________________________________.

**I need** _______________________________________.

**I need** _______________________________________.

**I need** _______________________________________.

**I need** _______________________________________.

**I need** _______________________________________.

**I need** _______________________________________.

**I need** _______________________________________.

**I need** _______________________________________.

**I need** _______________________________________.

**I need** _______________________________________.

# I CARE ABOUT...

Think about what and who you deeply **CARE ABOUT.**

Please complete the following:

**I care about**________________________________________________.

**I care about**________________________________________________.

**I care about**________________________________________________.

**I care about**________________________________________________.

**I care about**________________________________________________.

**I care about**________________________________________________.

**I care about**________________________________________________.

**I care about**________________________________________________.

**I care about**________________________________________________.

**I care about**________________________________________________.

**I care about**________________________________________________.

**I care about**________________________________________________.

**I care about**________________________________________________.

**I care about**________________________________________________.

**I care about**________________________________________________.

**I care about**________________________________________________.

**I care about**________________________________________________.

**I care about**________________________________________________.

**I care about**________________________________________________.

**I care about**________________________________________________.

**I care about**________________________________________________.

**I care about**________________________________________________.

**I care about**________________________________________________.

**I care about**________________________________________________.

# I DON'T CARE ABOUT…

Think about what you don't **CARE ABOUT.**

Please complete the following:

**I don't care about**_______________________________________________________.

**I don't care about**_______________________________________________________.

**I don't care about**_______________________________________________________.

**I don't care about**_______________________________________________________.

**I don't care about**_______________________________________________________.

**I don't care about**_______________________________________________________.

**I don't care about**_______________________________________________________.

**I don't care about**_______________________________________________________.

**I don't care about**_______________________________________________________.

**I don't care about**_______________________________________________________.

**I don't care about**_______________________________________________________.

**I don't care about**_______________________________________________________.

**I don't care about**_______________________________________________________.

**I don't care about**_______________________________________________________.

**I don't care about**_______________________________________________________.

**I don't care about**_______________________________________________________.

**I don't care about**_______________________________________________________.

**I don't care about**_______________________________________________________.

**I don't care about**_______________________________________________________.

**I don't care about**_______________________________________________________.

**I don't care about**_______________________________________________________.

**I don't care about**_______________________________________________________.

**I don't care about**_______________________________________________________.

**I don't care about**_______________________________________________________.

**I don't care about**_______________________________________________________.

**I don't care about**_______________________________________________________.

# I WANT TO BE ...

Think about what you **WANT TO BE**.

Please complete the following:

**I want to be** _______________________________________________ .

**I want to be** _______________________________________________ .

**I want to be** _______________________________________________ .

**I want to be** _______________________________________________ .

**I want to be** _______________________________________________ .

**I want to be** _______________________________________________ .

**I want to be** _______________________________________________ .

**I want to be** _______________________________________________ .

**I want to be** _______________________________________________ .

**I want to be** _______________________________________________ .

**I want to be** _______________________________________________ .

**I want to be** _______________________________________________ .

**I want to be** _______________________________________________ .

**I want to be** _______________________________________________ .

**I want to be** _______________________________________________ .

**I want to be** _______________________________________________ .

**I want to be** _______________________________________________ .

**I want to be** _______________________________________________ .

**I want to be** _______________________________________________ .

**I want to be** _______________________________________________ .

**I want to be** _______________________________________________ .

**I want to be** _______________________________________________ .

**I want to be** _______________________________________________ .

**I want to be** _______________________________________________ .

**I want to be** _______________________________________________ .

**I want to be** _______________________________________________ .

# ANGER, ADDICTION AND CONTROL

**We had felt angry at least once about something or someone. How do we cope with anger? How do we manage frustration, provocation, irritation, disappointment, stress, conflict, and resentment? How do we identify physical, emotional and cognitive cues that may trigger these feelings?**

**There is no doubt that uncontrollable anger can lead to legal problems and damage relationships. We must recognize what causes or triggers anger, and deal with emotional and physical pain without drugs or alcohol. We must identify what is hurting inside of us in a therapeutic environment, and learn to forgive and heal. We must enhance consciousness of angry feelings by nourishing acceptance and recognizing the advantages of understanding, and forgiving past hurtful situations. We must forgive ourselves and others, and with determination move forward. We must improve our inner and interpersonal relationships, and maintain a positive attitude. We must increase comprehension of our body, mind, and emotion patterns, and apply mindfulness and self-control.**

**How can we deal with anger without numbing it with drugs or alcohol?**

1.  When you are angry do you use drugs or alcohol? YES/NO. Please explain.

_______________________________________________________

_______________________________________________________

_______________________________________________________

2.  Do you feel angry after using drugs and alcohol? YES/NO. Please explain.

_______________________________________________________

_______________________________________________________

_______________________________________________________

3.  How do you manage your anger?

_______________________________________________________

_______________________________________________________

_______________________________________________________

4.  How do you know when you are angry? What happens to you physically, mentally, emotionally?

Pysically:_______________________________________________

Mentally:________________________________________________

Emotionally:_____________________________________________

Please indicate √ your symptoms of anger.

| **Physical Signs** | **Mental Signs** | **Emotional Signs** | **Behavior** |
|---|---|---|---|
| Rapid heart beat | Rage | Racing thoughts | Running |
| Stomach ache | Aggressive thoughts | Overwhelmed | Violent |
| Sweating palms | Irritation | Anxious | Pacing |
| Tense Muscles | Confusion | Sad | Yelling |
| Tight Chest | Shutdown | Depressed | Spiting |
| Hot neck/ face | Disorganized thoughts | Nervous | Swearing |
| Clenching jaws | Guilt | Harmful thoughts | Throwing |
| Clenching teeth | Shame | Other:___________ | Laughing |
| Dizziness | Lack of concentration | Other:___________ | Passive |
| Tingling | Fantasies | Other:___________ | Aggressive |
| Tight chest | Mood change | | Assertive |
| Shaking | Other:___________ | | Indifferent |
| Headache | Other:___________ | | Other:____ |
| Fatigue | | | Other:____ |
| Other:___________ | | | |

- **How difficult is for you to maintain self-control after having the above symptoms?**

```
___________________________________________________________
   0    1    2    3    4    5    6    7    8    9   10
Not Difficult                                      Very
                                                   Difficult
```

**Please explain how the symptoms you identified impact your life.**

___________________________________________________

___________________________________________________

___________________________________________________

___________________________________________________

___________________________________________________

___________________________________________________

5.  List the **FIRST** signs you have noticed when you start getting angry.

Pysically:_______________________________________________________

_______________________________________________________

Mentally:_______________________________________________________

_______________________________________________________

Emotionally:_______________________________________________________

_______________________________________________________

**6.**  What makes you angry?

_______________________________________________________

_______________________________________________________

_______________________________________________________

_______________________________________________________

7.  How do you react when you are angry? Please describe at least three past situations and how you reacted.

_______________________________________________________

_______________________________________________________

_______________________________________________________

_______________________________________________________

8.   Did you have legal issues because of your anger? YES/NO. Please describe past and present events.

_______________________________________________________

_______________________________________________________

_______________________________________________________

_______________________________________________________

9. What negative behaviors would you like to avoid when you are angry?

_______________________________________________________

_______________________________________________________

_______________________________________________________

_______________________________________________________

_______________________________________________________

_______________________________________________________

10.  What is your plan to control your anger?

_______________________________________________

_______________________________________________

_______________________________________________

_______________________________________________

11. Identify eighteen positive reactions that you may practice to control your anger.
    (e.g. walk away, exercise)

1._______________________________________________

2._______________________________________________

3._______________________________________________

4._______________________________________________

5._______________________________________________

6._______________________________________________

7._______________________________________________

8._______________________________________________

9._______________________________________________

10._______________________________________________

11._______________________________________________

12._______________________________________________

13._______________________________________________

14._______________________________________________

15._______________________________________________

16._______________________________________________

17._______________________________________________

18._______________________________________________

12.  **Please write below the people, things, places, and other stuff damaged or destroyed because of your anger.**

| | People<br>(e.g. partner) | Things<br>(e.g. T.V.) | Places<br>(e.g. apartment) | Other<br>(e.g. freedom) |
|---|---|---|---|---|
| 1. | | | | |
| 2. | | | | |
| 3. | | | | |
| 4. | | | | |
| 5. | | | | |
| 6. | | | | |
| 7. | | | | |
| 8. | | | | |
| 9. | | | | |
| 10. | | | | |
| 11. | | | | |
| 12. | | | | |

Please reflect, elaborate, and discuss what you wrote above.

_______________________________________________________________

_______________________________________________________________

_______________________________________________________________

_______________________________________________________________

_______________________________________________________________

_______________________________________________________________

_______________________________________________________________

_______________________________________________________________

_______________________________________________________________

_______________________________________________________________

_______________________________________________________________

# ANGER AND MOTIVATION

**The motivation to change comes from inside of us. Everything we do is motivated by something internal or external. Motivation is for human beings what fuel is for vehicles. Our desire to change may be influenced by internal understanding and grow by external and environmental factors. We are our true motivators when we honestly seek our true selves.**

**1. How motivated are you to Change? Please circle one.**

| 0 | 1 | 2 | 3 | 4 | 5 | 6 | 7 | 8 | 9 | 10 |
|---|---|---|---|---|---|---|---|---|---|----|

Not
Motivated

100% Motivated

1. Please explain your choice?

_________________________________________________

_________________________________________________

_________________________________________________

_________________________________________________

2. Please write at least three characteristics that you would you like to change about yourself in the next three months?

1._______________________________________________

_________________________________________________

2._______________________________________________

_________________________________________________

3._______________________________________________

_________________________________________________

3. What motivates you to learn how to control your anger? Please explain.

_________________________________________________

_________________________________________________

4. How will your life be if you choose to control your anger?

_________________________________________________

_________________________________________________

_________________________________________________

# ANGER AND IMPULSE REACTIONS

**Impulsive reactions, behaviors and attitudes, certainly can offend, disrespect, provoke and result in predicaments with ourselves, others, and ultimately generate legal problems.**

**1. Do you remember how impulsive you were as a child? Please circle one.**

| 0 | 1 | 2 | 3 | 4 | 5 | 6 | 7 | 8 | 9 | 10 + |
|---|---|---|---|---|---|---|---|---|---|------|

Not
Impulsive

Extremely Impulsive

Please explain your choice?

_______________________________________________

_______________________________________________

_______________________________________________

**2. How impulsive are you NOW? Please circle one.**

| 0 | 1 | 2 | 3 | 4 | 5 | 6 | 7 | 8 | 9 | 10 |
|---|---|---|---|---|---|---|---|---|---|----|

Not
Impulsive

Extremely Impulsive

Please explain your choice?

_______________________________________________

_______________________________________________

_______________________________________________

**3. How much trouble have you had because of impulse attitudes and behaviors? Please circle one.**

| 0 | 1 | 2 | 3 | 4 | 5 | 6 | 7 | 8 | 9 | 10 + |
|---|---|---|---|---|---|---|---|---|---|------|

None

A lot

Please explain your choice?

_______________________________________________

_______________________________________________

_______________________________________________

# ANGER, PEOPLE, PLACES, THINGS, EVENTS, THOUGHTS AND DESIRES

1.  Please identify what may drive you to express anger(check any of the following that may apply): √

| | | |
|---|---|---|
| ☐ Stress | ☐ Inferiority feelings | ☐ Provocation |
| ☐ Tension with others | ☐ Grief | ☐ Inability to make friends |
| ☐ Pain | ☐ Panic | ☐ People |
| ☐ Anxiety | ☐ Fears and phobias | ☐ Unhealthy relationships |
| ☐ Depression | ☐ Obsessions | ☐ Inability to have a good time/fun |
| ☐ Boredom | ☐ Loneliness | ☐ Places |
| ☐ Physical pain | ☐ Racing thoughts | ☐ Inability to make decisions |
| ☐ Lack of employment | ☐ Traumatic experiences | ☐ Disrespect |
| ☐ Constant sleepiness | ☐ Conflicts | ☐ Legal problems |
| ☐ Inability to relax | ☐ Probation | ☐ Financial problems |
| ☐ Insomnia | ☐ Parole | ☐ Gambling |
| ☐ Recurrent dreams | ☐ Homeless | ☐ Job problems |
| ☐ Nightmares | ☐ Sexual orientation | ☐ Inability to keep a job |
| ☐ Hallucinations | ☐ Sexual problems | ☐ Family problems |
| ☐ Mood swings | ☐ Medical problems | ☐ Other:_________ |
| ☐ Peer pressure | ☐ Unemployment:_______ | ☐ Other:_________ |

Other (Specify):

_______________________________________________

_______________________________________________

_______________________________________________

_______________________________________________

_______________________________________________

2.  Please explain your choices.

_______________________________________________

_______________________________________________

_______________________________________________

_______________________________________________

_______________________________________________

_______________________________________________

_______________________________________________

_______________________________________________

_______________________________________________

# ANGER, STRESS AND PLANNING ACTIVITIES

1.  Please choose √ the activities that you think will be most helpful to assist you in reducing your daily stress.

| | | |
|---|---|---|
| ☐ Meditating | ☐ Praying | ☐ Laughing |
| ☐ Journaling | ☐ Attending church | ☐ Partying |
| ☐ Finding hobbies | ☐ Attending bible study | ☐ Playing sports |
| ☐ Attending self-help meetings | ☐ Listening to music | ☐ Spending time with family |
| ☐ Attending AA meetings | ☐ Reading a book, magazine | ☐ Playing video games |
| ☐ Attending NA meetings | ☐ Watching TV | ☐ Helping others |
| ☐ Attending GA meetings | ☐ Going to the park | ☐ Eating your favorite food |
| ☐ Going to the gym | ☐ Going to the movies | ☐ Treating yourself with new stuff |
| ☐ Exercising with a friend | ☐ Gardening | ☐ Increasing romance |
| ☐ Exercising alone | ☐ Cleaning | ☐ Dating |
| ☐ Walking | ☐ Washing | ☐ Taking my partner out to dinner |
| ☐ Talking to a friend | ☐ Doing house chores | ☐ Practicing mindfulness |
| ☐ Talking to a family member | ☐ Going for a ride | ☐ Practicing Yoga |
| ☐ Talking to your sponsor | ☐ Shopping | ☐ Other:_______________ |
| ☐ Talking to your counselor | ☐ Attending school | ☐ Other: |

2.  Please explain in detail how the activities you chose √ will assist you to reduce stress.

_______________________________________________________________________

_______________________________________________________________________

_______________________________________________________________________

_______________________________________________________________________

_______________________________________________________________________

_______________________________________________________________________

_______________________________________________________________________

_______________________________________________________________________

_______________________________________________________________________

_______________________________________________________________________

_______________________________________________________________________

_______________________________________________________________________

_______________________________________________________________________

_______________________________________________________________________

# ANGER AND CHANGE

**We motivate ourselves by improving insight into our self-defeated, self-destructive attitudes and behaviors, and by genuinely retaining awareness of what we really want from life.**

**Are you determined to change your life for the better? Do you want to remain focus on the positive aspects of life? Can you motivate, educate, and empower yourself?  Are you ready to change and apply self-control? Are you confident about your abilities to remain free of conflict?**

**Can you? YES/NO Will you? YES/NO**

1.  Think about your **LAST** problem due to anger? What happened?

_______________________________________________________

_______________________________________________________

_______________________________________________________

_______________________________________________________

2.  What could you have **DONE** differently?

_______________________________________________________

_______________________________________________________

_______________________________________________________

_______________________________________________________

3.  How the conflict started?

_______________________________________________________

_______________________________________________________

_______________________________________________________

4.  **How many times did you promise yourself not to lose self-control? Please elaborate about situations that you lost self-control.**

| 0 | 1 | 2 | 3 | 4 | 5 | 6 | 7 | 8 | 9 | 10 | + |
|---|---|---|---|---|---|---|---|---|---|----|---|

_______________________________________________________

_______________________________________________________

_______________________________________________________

_______________________________________________________

5. What is going to be different **NOW**?

______________________________________________

______________________________________________

______________________________________________

______________________________________________

6. Have you been feeling frustrated, irritated, angry and impatient? YES/NO. Please explain.

______________________________________________

______________________________________________

______________________________________________

______________________________________________

7. Identify seven **SITUATIONS** you must avoid in order to remain free from anger.

1. _______________________________________

2. _______________________________________

3. _______________________________________

4. _______________________________________

5. _______________________________________

6. _______________________________________

7. _______________________________________

8. Identify five **PEOPLE** you must avoid in order to remain free from anger.

1._______________________________________

2._______________________________________

3._______________________________________

4._______________________________________

5._______________________________________

9.  Identify three **PLACES** you must avoid in order to remain free from anger.

1.______________________________________________________________

2.______________________________________________________________

3.______________________________________________________________

10. Identify three **DECISIONS** you must **MAKE DAILY** in order to remain free
    from anger.

1.______________________________________________________________

2.______________________________________________________________

3.______________________________________________________________

11. Identify three **HIGH RISK BEHAVIORS** you must avoid in order to remain
    free from anger.

1.______________________________________________________________

2.______________________________________________________________

3.______________________________________________________________

12. Identify the name of three **PEOPLE** you can reach for support when you feel
    angry.

1.______________________________________________________________

2.______________________________________________________________

3.______________________________________________________________

13. Identify four **HEALTHY** coping skills that you must use when you feel angry.

1.______________________________________________________________

2.______________________________________________________________

3.______________________________________________________________

4.______________________________________________________________

14. Identify five **UNHEALTHY** ways you must **AVOID** when you feel angry.

1.______________________________________________________

2.______________________________________________________

3.______________________________________________________

4.______________________________________________________

5.______________________________________________________

15. Identify the name of three **PLACES** you may go when you feel angry.

1.______________________________________________________

2.______________________________________________________

3.______________________________________________________

**16.** Identify three **PHYSICAL** signs of **STRESS** that may trigger your anger. Please explain. (e.g. headaches, sleep disruption, )

1.______________________________________________________

2.______________________________________________________

3.______________________________________________________

**17.** Identify three **EMOTIONAL** signs of **STRESS** that may trigger your anger. Please explain. (e.g. sadness, fear, pain, excessive worrying))

1.______________________________________________________

2.______________________________________________________

3.______________________________________________________

**18.** Identify three **MENTAL** signs of **STRESS** that may trigger your anger. Please explain. (e.g. lack of assertiveness, lack of confidence)

1.______________________________________________________

2.______________________________________________________

3.______________________________________________________

# ANGER AND LIFESTYLE

**A lifestyle is a way of living and a way of life with certain habits, attitudes, morals, principles, economic status, and other aspects that may shape an individual or a group. Sometimes people need to change everything in order to remain free of trouble. The changes may include employment, friendships, location, environment, diet, belief system, partnerships, relationships, and other aspects that have directly or indirectly impact on their lives.**

**You must change your lifestyle if it attracts trouble.**

1. Does your lifestyle attract trouble?  YES/NO. Please elaborate.

___________________________________________________________

___________________________________________________________

**2.  How motivated are you to change your LIFESTYLE? Please circle one.**

| 0 | 1 | 2 | 3 | 4 | 5 | 6 | 7 | 8 | 9 | 10 |
|---|---|---|---|---|---|---|---|---|---|---|

**Not Motivated**                                                                     **100% Motivated**

3. What do you **NEED** to change about your lifestyle?

___________________________________________________________

___________________________________________________________

4. What do you **WANT** to change about your lifestyle?

___________________________________________________________

___________________________________________________________

5. What **WOULD** you change about your lifestyle?

___________________________________________________________

___________________________________________________________

6. What **CAN** you change about your lifestyle?

___________________________________________________________

___________________________________________________________

7. What **MUST** you change about your lifestyle?

___________________________________________________________

___________________________________________________________

___________________________________________________________

# ANGER, STRESS AND WARNING SIGNS

**We change our normal way of living due to the demands of stress, and may feel physically, emotionally, mentally, and spiritually overwhelmed.**

**1.  When you are stressed, your mind is** ________________________________

| 0 | 1 | 2 | 3 | 4 | 5 | 6 | 7 | 8 | 9 | 10 |
|---|---|---|---|---|---|---|---|---|---|----|

**Clear Mind**

**Trouble Thinking Clear**

**Before your last anger outbursts**                                  Please circle one

| | |
|---|---|
| a)  Did you think about the same over and over? | YES/NO |
| b)  Did you dream about conflicts with others? | YES/NO |
| c)  Did you have mood swings? | YES/NO |
| d)  Did you have trouble remembering things? | YES/NO |
| e)  Did you have trouble managing daily stress? | YES/NO |
| f)  Did you feel shame or guilt? | YES/NO |
| g)  Did you feel easily frustrated and irritated? | YES/NO |
| h)  Did you feel hopeless, anxious, and depressed? | YES/NO |
| i)  Did you think past traumatic experiences? | YES/NO |
| j)  Did you think about the people who had hurt you? | YES/NO |
| k)  Did you perceive an offense or provocation towards you? | YES/NO |
| l)  Did you feel bored? | YES/NO |
| m)  Did you feel that you didn't care much about anything? | YES/NO |
| n)  Did you feel sorrow about your life? | YES/NO |
| o)  Did you feel that you were alone? | YES/NO |
| p)  Did you feel that you didn't have any alternatives but fight? | YES/NO |
| q)  Did you feel you were in a trap? | YES/NO |
| r)  Did you neglect healthy habits? | YES/NO |
| t)  Did you feel social pressure? | YES/NO |
| u)  Did you have any changes on your sleeping patterns? | YES/NO |
| v)  Did you feel that you needed to have more fun? | YES/NO |
| w)  Were you in the company of friends? | YES/NO |

Please complete

Before my last anger outbursts I_______________________________________________

________________________________________________________________

________________________________________________________________

________________________________________________________________

2. How many questions have you answered: YES____________ NO____________
   Reflect and explain your answers.

_______________________________________________________________________

_______________________________________________________________________

_______________________________________________________________________

_______________________________________________________________________

_______________________________________________________________________

_______________________________________________________________________

_______________________________________________________________________

_______________________________________________________________________

_______________________________________________________________________

_______________________________________________________________________


3. How do you react to stress?


**Physically:** (e.g. Lack of energy, sleep disturbances)

_______________________________________________________________________

_______________________________________________________________________

_______________________________________________________________________

_______________________________________________________________________


**Emotionally/Mentally:** (e.g. irritability, nervousness, edginess)

_______________________________________________________________________

_______________________________________________________________________

_______________________________________________________________________

_______________________________________________________________________

_______________________________________________________________________

**Behaviorally:** (e.g. angry outbursts, less sleep)

_______________________________________________

_______________________________________________

_______________________________________________

_______________________________________________

_______________________________________________

_______________________________________________


4.  Identify your daily, weekly, monthly, yearly stressors.

**Daily:**

_______________________________________________

_______________________________________________

_______________________________________________

Explain: ________________________________________

_______________________________________________

_______________________________________________

_______________________________________________

_______________________________________________

**Weekly:**

_______________________________________________

_______________________________________________

_______________________________________________

Explain: ________________________________________

_______________________________________________

_______________________________________________

_______________________________________________

**Monthly:**

___________________________________________________

___________________________________________________

___________________________________________________

___________________________________________________

Explain: _____________________________________________

___________________________________________________

___________________________________________________

___________________________________________________

**Yearly:**

___________________________________________________

___________________________________________________

___________________________________________________

___________________________________________________

Explain: _____________________________________________

___________________________________________________

___________________________________________________

___________________________________________________

5. How can you **MANAGE** stress? Please identify at least seven ways you can manage and reduce stress. (e.g. plan your time, prioritize, organize, exercise, speak with a friend, apply relaxation and meditation techniques)

1. _________________________________________________

2. _________________________________________________

3. _________________________________________________

4. _________________________________________________

5. _________________________________________________

6. _________________________________________________

7. _________________________________________________

# ANGER, LIES, FEARS AND MANIPULATION

**Fears, manipulation, and deception may generate conflicts and anger. We must understand the roots of conflicts that may arise from differences. We must be aware of our needs, and figure out why we are truly in conflict with ourselves and others. Conflict must encourage us to examine issues wisely and inspire solutions. The turmoil of our values, perceptions, desires, ideas, morals, beliefs, attitudes, and tendencies are fuel for our conflicts. When in conflict with others, we must be mindful of our emotions and behaviors, and try to comprehend the emotions and behaviors of others, in a calm, relaxed, consistent, fair and alert way. We must pay attention to nonverbal communication and entertain win/win resolutions.**

1. Have you been in trouble because of a conflict with a person? (e.g. your partner) YES/NO. Please explain.

________________________________________________________

________________________________________________________

________________________________________________________

________________________________________________________

________________________________________________________

2. Have you been in conflict with your inner self? (e.g. daily contradictions, struggle with decisions) YES/NO. Please explain.

________________________________________________________

________________________________________________________

________________________________________________________

________________________________________________________

3. Do you feel uncomfortable, stressed, or agitated when you are in conflict with yourself or others? YES/NO. Please explain.

________________________________________________________

________________________________________________________

________________________________________________________

________________________________________________________

________________________________________________________

4.  Are you able to think about positive outcomes when in conflict with others?
    YES/NO. Please explain.

_______________________________________________________________________

_______________________________________________________________________

_______________________________________________________________________

_______________________________________________________________________

_______________________________________________________________________

5.  How do you resolve a conflict with somebody? Do you effectively listen? Do you
    reflect about what is being said or done to resolve the conflict? Please explain
    how you have resolved a personal conflict?

_______________________________________________________________________

_______________________________________________________________________

_______________________________________________________________________

_______________________________________________________________________

_______________________________________________________________________

_______________________________________________________________________

_______________________________________________________________________

6.  When in conflict with others, do you clarify, acknowledge, discuss, and establish
    common goals that are beneficial to both parties? YES/NO. Please illustrate by
    explaining a conflict you have had in the past.

_______________________________________________________________________

_______________________________________________________________________

_______________________________________________________________________

_______________________________________________________________________

_______________________________________________________________________

7.  Are you able to identify barriers to resolve a conflict, and in a positive, calm way, agree about how to resolve the conflict? YES/NO. Please illustrate by explaining a conflict you have had.

_______________________________________________

_______________________________________________

_______________________________________________

_______________________________________________

_______________________________________________

_______________________________________________

_______________________________________________

8.  Would you take responsibility and accountability for a conflict? YES/NO. Please illustrate by explaining a conflict that had a resolution.

_______________________________________________

_______________________________________________

_______________________________________________

_______________________________________________

_______________________________________________

_______________________________________________

_______________________________________________

**9. How capable are you in finding a RESOLUTION for a conflict without breaking the law?**

**Please circle one**

| 0 | 1 | 2 | 3 | 4 | 5 | 6 | 7 | 8 | 9 | 10 |
|---|---|---|---|---|---|---|---|---|---|---|
| **Not capable** | | | | | | | | | | **Extremely capable** |

Please explain your answer:

_______________________________________________

_______________________________________________

_______________________________________________

_______________________________________________

# RELATIONSHIPS

**Relationships are necessary in our society. Healthy relationships have a great impact in the prevention of conflict. We may or may not have a healthy relationship with ourselves, our family, our co-workers, or with our partner. Our perceptions about our healthy or unhealthy relationships may vary with our belief system and the level of acceptance or denial. Unhealthy relationships sometimes deliver enough force of shame, guilt, frustration, pain, resentment, and annoyance to give up harmony and hope. A healthy connection between people must be based on mutual respect, trust, loyalty, good communication, honesty, and a sense of own identity and care.**

1. In your opinion, what makes a healthy relationship? (e.g. mutual respect)

______________________________________________________________

______________________________________________________________

______________________________________________________________

2. In your opinion, what makes an unhealthy relationship? (e.g. attempt to control or manipulate others)

______________________________________________________________

______________________________________________________________

______________________________________________________________

3. What makes a healthy romantic relationship? Please choose √ what you agree.

Write other

| | | | | | | |
|---|---|---|---|---|---|---|
| ☐ | **Fairness** | ☐ | **Support** | ☐ | **Ability to express** | ☐ ______ |
| ☐ | **Love** | ☐ | **Consistency** | ☐ | **No violence** | ☐ ______ |
| ☐ | **Arguments** | ☐ | **Good communication** | ☐ | **Feeling of safety** | ☐ ______ |
| ☐ | **Mental stress** | ☐ | **Sincerity** | ☐ | **No fear** | ☐ ______ |
| ☐ | **Instigation** | ☐ | **Honesty** | ☐ | **Appreciation** | ☐ ______ |
| ☐ | **Nagging** | ☐ | **Mutual respect** | ☐ | **Care** | ☐ ______ |
| ☐ | **Gossip** | ☐ | **Humor** | ☐ | **Connection** | ☐ ______ |
| ☐ | **Over reaction** | ☐ | **Sense of identity** | ☐ | **Happiness** | ☐ ______ |
| ☐ | **Silence** | ☐ | **Validation** | ☐ | **Use of drugs** | ☐ ______ |

**Please discuss your choices with your therapist or in group.**

**Please choose if you agree or disagree with statements**

**When I am in a romantic relationship**

| | | | | |
|---|---|---|---|---|
| 1. | I care only about myself | | AGREE | DISAGREE |
| 2. | I feel secure and appreciated | | AGREE | DISAGREE |
| 3. | I don't laugh much or feel happy | | AGRRE | DISAGREE |
| 4. | I have weekly arguments | | AGREE | DISAGREE |
| 5. | I use drugs with my partner | | AGREE | DISAGREE |
| 6. | I usually attempt to control and manipulate | | AGREE | DISAGREE |
| 7. | I feel pressure to please my partner all the time | | AGREE | DISAGREE |
| 8. | I have a lack of privacy | | AGREE | DISAGREE |
| 9. | I feel controlled and victimized | | AGREE | DISAGREE |
| 10. | I am unable to work or be independent | | AGREE | DISAGREE |
| 11. | I have limited access to my family | | AGREE | DISAGREE |
| 12. | I don't have too many friendships | | AGREE | DISAGREE |
| 13. | I worry about my future | | AGREE | DISAGREE |
| 14. | I don't make too many decisions | | AGREE | DISAGREE |
| 15. | I lack confidence about my future | | AGREE | DISAGREE |
| 16. | I am happy | | AGREE | DISAGREE |
| 17. | I respect my partner | | AGREE | DISAGREE |
| 18. | I trust my partner | | AGREE | DISAGREE |
| 19. | I am loyal to my partner | | AGREE | DISAGREE |
| 20. | I have affairs | | AGREE | DISAGREE |
| 21. | I don't trust my partner | | AGREE | DISAGREE |
| 22. | I hide my drugs and alcohol from my partner | | AGREE | DISAGREE |
| 23. | I feel lonely | | AGREE | DISAGREE |
| 24. | I am overwhelmed | | AGREE | DISAGREE |
| 25. | I break the law and get involved with the legal system | | AGREE | DISAGREE |

**Please discuss your answers with your therapist or in group.**

# THE IMPORTANCE OF A BALANCED LIFE

**A balanced life is a life well lived. We seek balance in so many aspects of our lives because we want to feel free of stress, and enjoy the elements of this world with a clear mind set. We must look at our life and fully understand its blue print, purpose and direction. We must assess our goals, plans, and objectives and reflect about how to accomplish them by balancing external (e.g. work, family, friendships, responsibilities) and internal (e.g. health, mind, gratification, self-reward) forces. Our true happiness is always shaped by balance.**

**We must empower and motivate ourselves in order to be free of conflicts. Let go of worries and keep feeding joy and harmony into your life.**

1.  Is your life balanced? YES/NO. Please explain.

_______________________________________________________________

_______________________________________________________________

_______________________________________________________________

_______________________________________________________________

_______________________________________________________________

_______________________________________________________________

2.  How balanced do you feel with your family time? Do you spend enough time with your family? YES/NO. Please explain.

_______________________________________________________________

_______________________________________________________________

_______________________________________________________________

_______________________________________________________________

_______________________________________________________________

_______________________________________________________________

3.  Do you spend enough time by yourself? YES/NO. Please explain.

_______________________________________________________________

_______________________________________________________________

_______________________________________________________________

_______________________________________________________________

_______________________________________________________________

_______________________________________________________________

4.  How do you motivate yourself?

____________________________________________________________

____________________________________________________________

____________________________________________________________

____________________________________________________________

____________________________________________________________

5.  What should you do to balance your life?

____________________________________________________________

____________________________________________________________

____________________________________________________________

____________________________________________________________

6.  What activities must you decrease or increase in order to find balance in your life?
    Please explain.

____________________________________________________________

____________________________________________________________

____________________________________________________________

____________________________________________________________

7.  What can you do in one week to initiate the process of balancing your life?

____________________________________________________________

____________________________________________________________

____________________________________________________________

____________________________________________________________

8.  Are you able to connect with your inner self and enjoy life? YES/NO. Please explain.

______________________________________________________________

______________________________________________________________

______________________________________________________________

______________________________________________________________

9.  Who can help you to find balance in your life?

______________________________________________________________

______________________________________________________________

______________________________________________________________

10. Name at least 5 healthy ways to increase balance in your life.

    **1.**______________________________________________________

    **2.**______________________________________________________

    **3.**______________________________________________________

    **4.**______________________________________________________

    **5.**______________________________________________________

- **How BALANCED is your life today?**

**Please circle one**

| 0 | 1 | 2 | 3 | 4 | 5 | 6 | 7 | 8 | 9 | 10 |
|---|---|---|---|---|---|---|---|---|---|---|
| Not balanced | | | | | Half balanced | | | | | Extremely balanced |

**Please explain your choice.**

______________________________________________________________

______________________________________________________________

______________________________________________________________

______________________________________________________________

______________________________________________________________

# MINDFULNESS IS NOW

**Mindfulness is the state of being conscious, completely awake, and fully attentive to the internal and external elements of the present moment. When we are awake from our daily automatic life, we start living what appears to be a surreal dimension of reality. We understand and appreciate the interconnection of everything without judging or falling for life distractions (e.g. politics, sports, organized religion). We have insight and we are insight of the present moment. When we achieve a sublime mindfulness approach to life, we experience great freedom and quality of living. We are no longer conditioned to act and react on auto-pilot. We make wiser choices because we are _awake_. The practice of mindfulness assists us to identify and increase self- control and awareness of impulsive, automatically destructive, addictive, risky behaviors.**

1. Do you have awareness of your thoughts, attitudes and behaviors that may lead to anger outbursts? YES/NO. Please explain.

\
\
\
\
\
\

2. Have you decided in an automatic and impulsive way when you act angry? YES/NO. Please elaborate about past situations.

\
\
\
\
\

3. Are you able to pause, recognize, and challenge emotional and physical experiences that may lead to anger outbursts? YES/NO. Please explain.

\
\
\
\
\

4. Are you able to pause, acknowledge, understand, and be nonjudgmental towards yourself and your experiences? YES/NO. Please explain.

_______________________________________________

_______________________________________________

_______________________________________________

_______________________________________________

_______________________________________________

5. Are you always conscious of your emotions, actions, reactions and behaviors? YES/NO. Please explain.

_______________________________________________

_______________________________________________

_______________________________________________

_______________________________________________

_______________________________________________

_______________________________________________

6. What can you do to remain focused and attentive to your anger?

_______________________________________________

_______________________________________________

_______________________________________________

_______________________________________________

**7. How much mindful / aware are you right NOW?**

**Please circle one**

| **0** | **1** | **2** | **3** | **4** | **5** | **6** | **7** | **8** | **9** | **10** |
|---|---|---|---|---|---|---|---|---|---|---|
| **Not at all** | | | | | | | | | | **Extremely** |

**Please explain your answer:**

_______________________________________________

_______________________________________________

_______________________________________________

_______________________________________________

_______________________________________________

# ALWAYS MINDFULNESS

Please circle

| | | | |
|---|---|---|---|
| 1. | Do you find it hard to pay attention to the things you say or do? | YES | NO |
| 2. | Have you got in trouble because of your impulsive decisions? | YES | NO |
| 3. | Do you have difficulty paying attention during tasks? | YES | NO |
| 4. | Do you multi-task? | YES | NO |
| 5. | Do you act before you think of the consequences? | YES | NO |
| 6. | Are you worried about the future or the past? | YES | NO |
| 7. | Do you tend to forget daily responsibilities? | YES | NO |
| 8. | Do you have difficulty enjoying the present moment? | YES | NO |
| 9. | Do you have fun with friends? | YES | NO |
| 10. | Are you able to relax? | YES | NO |
| 11. | Are you easily distracted by the media? | YES | NO |
| 12. | Do you sometimes forget about your responsibilities? | YES | NO |
| 13. | Are you easily influence by others? | YES | NO |
| 14. | Have you got in trouble in due to peer pressure? | YES | NO |
| 15. | Do you try to enjoy every moment of the day? | YES | NO |
| 16. | Are you attentive to what is happening NOW? | YES | NO |

**Please reflect, elaborate, and discuss your answers.**

_______________________________________________

_______________________________________________

_______________________________________________

_______________________________________________

_______________________________________________

_______________________________________________

_______________________________________________

_______________________________________________

_______________________________________________

# MAKING DECISIONS

**Any decision we make is ultimately our decision. Every day we make wise, average, or poor decisions. Every morning we decide to move on with our daily routine or do something different. Sometimes we decide things without much thinking, and sometimes we pause and think about what will be the best decision. We may move automatically like every other day, or we may reflect about the decision to make. Decision making may be facilitated by emotional, physical, or spiritual experiences, by measuring options and consequences, by perception of pros and cons, by acquiring brainstorming knowledge, by revising and reviewing, by describing and planning, and by values, needs, attitudes, and behaviors.**

1.  You decided to learn anger management. What makes this decision **NECESSARY** for you? Please explain your answer.

_______________________________________________

_______________________________________________

_______________________________________________

_______________________________________________

_______________________________________________

_______________________________________________

2.  You decided to pursue your personal goals, desires and dreams with a clear-headed mind, and focus on your self-control. What are the **BENEFITS** of this decision? Please explain your answer.

_______________________________________________

_______________________________________________

_______________________________________________

_______________________________________________

_______________________________________________

_______________________________________________

3.  What were the most difficult decisions you have made when you lacked self-control? What were the **CONSEQUENCES**? Please explain your answer.

_______________________________________________

_______________________________________________

_______________________________________________

_______________________________________________

_______________________________________________

_______________________________________________

4.  What was the most irrational decision you have made when you were in conflict with others? What were the **CONSEQUENCES**? Please explain your answer.

_______________________________________________________________

_______________________________________________________________

_______________________________________________________________

_______________________________________________________________

_______________________________________________________________

_______________________________________________________________

5.  Please write seven decisions you made when you were in a relationship, and how those decisions **AFFECTED** your life.

**1.** ___________________________________________________________

**2.** ___________________________________________________________

**3.** ___________________________________________________________

**4.** ___________________________________________________________

**5.** ___________________________________________________________

**6.** ___________________________________________________________

**7.** ___________________________________________________________

6.  Would you make the same decisions NOW? Please elaborate.

_______________________________________________________________

_______________________________________________________________

_______________________________________________________________

_______________________________________________________________

_______________________________________________________________

_______________________________________________________________

_______________________________________________________________

7.  Please write seven **UNHEALTHY** choices you made when you were in a relationship, which resulted in consequences that you did **NOT EXPECT**. Please explain.

1.________________________________________________________________

2.________________________________________________________________

3.________________________________________________________________

4.________________________________________________________________

5.________________________________________________________________

6.________________________________________________________________

7.________________________________________________________________

8.  Would you make the same choices **NOW?**  Please explain.

_________________________________________________________________

_________________________________________________________________

_________________________________________________________________

_________________________________________________________________

_________________________________________________________________

9.  How many times have your **IMPULSIVE** decisions resulted in legal problems? Please explain.

_________________________________________________________________

_________________________________________________________________

_________________________________________________________________

_________________________________________________________________

_________________________________________________________________

10. How many times have your **THOUGHTFUL** decisions resulted in conflict with others? Please explain.

_________________________________________________________________

_________________________________________________________________

_________________________________________________________________

_________________________________________________________________

_________________________________________________________________

11. What are the **PROS and CONS** of making a decision after carefully calculating
the consequences? Please explain.

_______________________________________________________________

_______________________________________________________________

_______________________________________________________________

_______________________________________________________________

12. **How do you make a choice or a decision?** Write an example of a decision you
made today, and explain in detail why and how you came to that decision. Please
write the consequences of your decision, pros and cons, and possible alternatives.

_______________________________________________________________

_______________________________________________________________

_______________________________________________________________

_______________________________________________________________

_______________________________________________________________

_______________________________________________________________

_______________________________________________________________

**13. How capable are you of making WISE and beneficial decisions?**

**Please circle one**

| 0 | 1 | 2 | 3 | 4 | 5 | 6 | 7 | 8 | 9 | 10 |
|---|---|---|---|---|---|---|---|---|---|---|

**Not
capable**

**Extremely
capable**

**Please explain your answer.**

_______________________________________________________________

_______________________________________________________________

_______________________________________________________________

_______________________________________________________________

_______________________________________________________________

_______________________________________________________________

# SOLVING PROBLEMS

**We will encounter problems during our lives. Sometimes we will have minor problems, and sometimes unthinkable problems. Problems exist, and we are able to resolve them by first identifying symptoms of the problem, seeking information about the problem, brainstorming answers for the problem, choosing the most beneficial resolution for the problem, visualizing and clarifying a plan to resolve the problem, reviewing the proposal to resolve the problem, and putting in action the most positive solution for the problem.**

1. When does a **SYMPTOM** of a problem become a problem? (*e.g. symptom-considering arguing with your partner about something*)

______________________________________________________________

______________________________________________________________

______________________________________________________________

2. Are you able to understand symptoms of your personal issues before they become **UNMANAGEABLE** problems? Please write about a problem you had and how you dealt with it.

______________________________________________________________

______________________________________________________________

______________________________________________________________

______________________________________________________________

3. Usually, do you **RESOLVE** your problems by yourself, or do you ask for help? Please explain by using an example of a problem you are currently facing.

______________________________________________________________

______________________________________________________________

______________________________________________________________

______________________________________________________________

4. Do you **MINIMIZE** your problems? Do you make your problems smaller than they are? YES/NO. Please explain.

______________________________________________________________

______________________________________________________________

______________________________________________________________

______________________________________________________________

**5.** Please list five **PROBLEMS** caused by your anger.

1.______________________________________________________________

2.______________________________________________________________

3.______________________________________________________________

4.______________________________________________________________

5.______________________________________________________________

**6.** Please list five ways in which you attempted to **CONVINCE** others that you did not have a problem with anger.

1.______________________________________________________________

2.______________________________________________________________

3.______________________________________________________________

4.______________________________________________________________

5.______________________________________________________________

7. Are you **NOW** aware of the impact of the problems caused by your anger and how it affected you and the people who care about you? YES/NO. In detail, clarify the impact of the problems caused by your anger.

______________________________________________________________

______________________________________________________________

______________________________________________________________

______________________________________________________________

______________________________________________________________

**8. How capable are you in resolving your problems?**

**Please circle one**

| **0** | **1** | **2** | **3** | **4** | **5** | **6** | **7** | **8** | **9** | **10**  **+** |
|---|---|---|---|---|---|---|---|---|---|---|
| **Not capable** | | | | | | | | | | **Extremely capable** |

**Please explain your answer:** ______________________________________

______________________________________________________________

# SPIRITUAL JOURNEY

How we view our own existence in the universe is what makes us aware of our actions and reactions to everything. Our physical existence constantly reinvents its time and connects our bodies and souls to the universe. We are the energy that the universe uses to magically and patiently evolve through us. Our bodies are a process that never stands still, and our souls are vessels seeking enlightenment by connecting and feeling the world physically, socially, emotionally, and spiritually.

Our souls constantly animate our bodies and seek balance, harmony, meaning, serenity, purpose, self-actualization, and satisfaction. We are the mindfulness conscience that brings change by letting go of our old limited beliefs. We meditate and seek positive change in our inner selves by embracing our body and soul towards the awakening of compassion, empathy, goodness, and love. We are souls that use bodies. We belong to the multi-level dimensions of the universe.

1.   How do you view your own spiritual existence in the universe?
     Please circle one.

| 0 | 1 | 2 | 3 | 4 | 5 | 6 | 7 | 8 | 9 | 10 |
|---|---|---|---|---|---|---|---|---|---|---|
| Do not | | | | | | | | | | Extremely |

**Some Spiritual Principles:**

| | | | |
|---|---|---|---|
| Honesty | Gratitude | Tolerance | Love |
| Acceptance | Forgiveness | Give more | Care |
| Surrender | Patience | Except less | Compassion |
| Accept Change | Live simple | Live humbly | Self-actualization |

2.   What do you think gives meaning to your life?

_______________________________________________

_______________________________________________

_______________________________________________

_______________________________________________

3.   Do you consider yourself spiritual? YES/NO. Please explain.

_______________________________________________

_______________________________________________

_______________________________________________

_______________________________________________

4.  If YES, how important is your spiritual belief? Please explain.

_______________________________________________________________

_______________________________________________________________

_______________________________________________________________

5.  Have you ever had a spiritual awakening? YES/NO. Please describe.

_______________________________________________________________

_______________________________________________________________

_______________________________________________________________

6.  Do you talk about spirituality or religion with someone? YES/NO. If, yes, who
    and when?

_______________________________________________________________

_______________________________________________________________

_______________________________________________________________

7.  Do you believe that spiritual and religious practices enhance the functioning of
    the brain in ways that improve physical and emotional health? YES/NO. Please
    explain.

_______________________________________________________________

_______________________________________________________________

_______________________________________________________________

_______________________________________________________________

8.  Do you think that contemplation about God and other spiritual values awakens
    our conscience and enhances the sensory perceptions about the Self?
    YES/NO. Please explain.

_______________________________________________________________

_______________________________________________________________

_______________________________________________________________

_______________________________________________________________

9.  Think about your body and how it works. Write about a physical illness that you
    have experienced and the events that followed.

_______________________________________________________________

_______________________________________________________________

_______________________________________________________________

_______________________________________________________________

_______________________________________________________________

_______________________________________________________________

10. Do you attend self-help groups? YES/NO. Please explain.

_______________________________________________________________

_______________________________________________________________

_______________________________________________________________

_______________________________________________________________

11.  Are you conscious or aware of the impact of anger on your body, mind, and soul? YES/NO. Please explain.

_______________________________________________________________

_______________________________________________________________

_______________________________________________________________

_______________________________________________________________

12. Are you able to practice mindfulness meditation by putting aside thoughts of the past and future, and staying in the present moment? YES/NO. Please explain.

_______________________________________________________________

_______________________________________________________________

_______________________________________________________________

_______________________________________________________________

13. Are you interested in learning more about meditation and relaxation techniques? YES/NO. If you answered yes, explain how beneficial it will be for you to know more about meditation and relaxation techniques.

_______________________________________________________________

_______________________________________________________________

_______________________________________________________________

_______________________________________________________________

_______________________________________________________________

**Discuss with your psychotherapist, ways to obtain information and learn more about meditation and relaxation techniques. You will enjoy a unique self-reflection experience, by cleansing your mind from accumulated thoughts.**

**The mind, soul and body are uniquely designed to be in harmony with each other, and through meditation, we are able to travel into a mindfulness conscience in a clear, wiser, focused, and profound way.**

# WORDS AND ACTIONS

Be not afraid of life. Always believe in yourself.

I thought about this statement when shaping many of my thoughts, and attitudes. My inner voice built confidence and assured me that life is worth living. We must appreciate a life of value, confidence, determination, courage, virtue, and understand that fear only exists to be conquered. Fear may become the greatest fertilizer to intensify our personal success.

We can, and we will conquer our fears by BELIEVING and KNOWING ourselves.


## WHAT YOU ARE AND WHAT YOU ARE SUPPOSED TO BE

We are what we think, and our thoughts can be believable to us and others. We have a blue print to follow and determine where our life must go. We are to see our lives not as an idea of living, but as a reality to accomplish. Our dreams, plans, and goals have more reasons for us to pursue them, than to let them fade away. We must embrace basic principles and deeply believe in ourselves.


## CHANGE

Change is not always wanted, accepted, or respected. We must connect with our emotions in order to understand our actions, and modify our behaviors. We must not ignore our needs to avoid changing our destructive behaviors. We must not forget the execution of forgiveness to avoid change.

Change is what connects the universe, and we are part of it. Accept, embrace, and understand that change is a beneficial element of life.

# GRIEF AND LOSS

Life sometimes brings us unthinkable pain due to grief and loss. We may lose a loved one, a close relationship, a pet, a friend, a job, a lover, our own health, or something or someone we care a lot for. We may feel angry, depressed, anxious, and dreamlike. We may avoid feelings of sadness and despair by taking the path of denial, which may result in substance abuse, mental illness, and health problems. We neglect ourselves and others, and question our ways mentally and spiritually. We may feel lost in the realm wheel of magic, test the boundaries of sanity, and our capacity to remain human.

Loss may change our ways of thinking, and generate emotions and physical reactions that we have never experienced.

Grief is a natural reaction to loss. Grief can take away our sense of belonging to something or someone, and we may feel sad, scared, and lonely. People grieve differently, depending on their life experiences, personality traits, faith, learned coping skills, support system, type of loss, or other factors.

Any loss can cause grief including:

- Death of a loved one
- Loss of a relationship
- Loss of own physical or mental health
- Loss of work or job
- Loss of financial stability
- Loss of possessions or property
- Loss of a loved place or stable home
- Loss of a child moving away

- An injury or disability
- Loss of a friend
- Loss of a lifestyle
- Miscarriage
- Loss of a plan or dream
- Loss of safety
- Loss of faith
- Other_______________________

By grieving we naturally accept loss, and heal by expressing our feelings and utilizing our support system. Do not be afraid to ask for help. Do not limit your tears. You must feel to heal.

We must start the healing process by acknowledging the roots of pain, and conquer the abysm of suffering.

The death of a loved one might encourage you to assess your own feelings about mortality. Grief and loss are personal and we must understand our emotions, seek our support system, and feel the natural process of healing without any resistance or delay.

1.  Please reflect on who or what you have lost during your life.

_______________________________________________________

_______________________________________________________

_______________________________________________________

_______________________________________________________

_______________________________________________________

_______________________________________________________

2.  Please list the emotions, thoughts and body changes you have had since your loss.

_______________________________________________________

_______________________________________________________

_______________________________________________________

_______________________________________________________

_______________________________________________________

_______________________________________________________

3.  How has your loss affected your social life?

_______________________________________________________

_______________________________________________________

_______________________________________________________

4.  How has your loss affected your self-respect?

_______________________________________________________

_______________________________________________________

_______________________________________________________

_______________________________________________________

5.  How has your loss affected your behaviors?

6.  How has your loss affected your relationships?

7.  Did you use drugs or alcohol because of the death of a love one? YES/NO. Please explain.

8.  Did you have difficulty dealing with emotions and thoughts of loss? YES/NO. Please explain.

# MY FUTURE BELONGS TO ME

**Summarize your plans and goals to maintain self-control and meet your needs.**

## TO IMPROVE THE RELATIONSHIP WITH MYSELF

I will________________________________________________________

________________________________________________________

________________________________________________________

________________________________________________________

## TO FIND OR MAINTAIN EMPLOYMENT

I will________________________________________________________

________________________________________________________

________________________________________________________

________________________________________________________

## TO FIND OR MAINTAIN HOUSING

I will________________________________________________________

________________________________________________________

________________________________________________________

________________________________________________________

## TO PURSUE EDUCATION OR VOCATIONAL SKILLS

I will________________________________________________________

________________________________________________________

________________________________________________________

________________________________________________________

## TO HANDLE URGES AND CRAVINGS

I will________________________________________________________

________________________________________________________

________________________________________________________

________________________________________________________

**TO HAVE OR MAINTAIN MEANS OF TRANSPORTATION**

I will_______________________________________________________________

_____________________________________________________________________

_____________________________________________________________________


**TO GAIN OR MAINTAIN A HEALTHY RELATIONSHIP WITH FAMILY**

I will_______________________________________________________________

_____________________________________________________________________

_____________________________________________________________________


**TO GAIN OR MAINTAIN A HEALTHY RELATIONSHIP WITH FRIENDS**

I will_______________________________________________________________

_____________________________________________________________________

_____________________________________________________________________


**TO LEARN MORE ABOUT MYSELF AND LIFE IN GENERAL**

I will_______________________________________________________________

_____________________________________________________________________

_____________________________________________________________________


**TO HAVE FUN AND ENJOY LIFE FREE OF CONFLICTS**

I will_______________________________________________________________

_____________________________________________________________________

_____________________________________________________________________


**TO REGULARLY UTILIZE MY SUPPORT SYSTEM**

I will_______________________________________________________________

_____________________________________________________________________

_____________________________________________________________________

**TO GAIN, MAINTAIN, AND EXPAND A HEALTHY SOCIAL NETWORK**

I will______________________________________________________________

______________________________________________________________

______________________________________________________________

______________________________________________________________


**TO REDUCE STRESS**

I will______________________________________________________________

______________________________________________________________

______________________________________________________________

______________________________________________________________


**TO ELIMINATE CHAOS IN MY LIFE**

I will______________________________________________________________

______________________________________________________________

______________________________________________________________

______________________________________________________________


**TO INCREASE RESPONSIBILITY FOR MY ACTIONS**

I will______________________________________________________________

______________________________________________________________

______________________________________________________________

______________________________________________________________


**TO APPLY PAUSE BEFORE REACTING**

I will______________________________________________________________

______________________________________________________________

______________________________________________________________

______________________________________________________________

**TO RECOGNIZE CONFLICTS**

I will______________________________________________________________

______________________________________________________________

______________________________________________________________

______________________________________________________________

______________________________________________________________


*Please add.*

TO ______________________________________________________________

I will______________________________________________________________

______________________________________________________________

______________________________________________________________

______________________________________________________________

______________________________________________________________

______________________________________________________________

______________________________________________________________


TO ______________________________________________________________

I will______________________________________________________________

______________________________________________________________

______________________________________________________________

______________________________________________________________

______________________________________________________________


TO ______________________________________________________________

I will______________________________________________________________

______________________________________________________________

______________________________________________________________

______________________________________________________________

______________________________________________________________

______________________________________________________________

# IDENTIFYING MY ISSUES AND BUILDING MY OWN PLANS

| | Describe problem symptoms/behaviors/ attitudes/addictions/ obsessions/compulsions and other matters that you would like to change | How you will resolve/change/improve /eliminate? By doing what?<br><br>Short Term Goals | Time Frame<br><br>How long will it take to achieve the Short Term Goals? | How you will resolve/change/improve /eliminate? By doing what?<br><br>Long Term Goals | Time Frame<br><br>How long will take to achieve Long Term Goals? |
|---|---|---|---|---|---|
| 1. | | | | | |
| 2. | | | | | |
| 3. | | | | | |
| 4. | | | | | |
| 5. | | | | | |
| 6. | | | | | |
| 7. | | | | | |

1.  Please elaborate about the benefits of your short and long-term goals, and current
    achievements.

_______________________________________________________________

_______________________________________________________________

_______________________________________________________________

_______________________________________________________________

_______________________________________________________________

_______________________________________________________________

_______________________________________________________________

_______________________________________________________________

_______________________________________________________________

_______________________________________________________________

2.  Who can you ask to help you achieve your goals?

_______________________________________________________________

_______________________________________________________________

_______________________________________________________________

_______________________________________________________________

- **How CONFIDENT are you in achieving your short and long term goals?**
**Please circle one.**

| 0 | 1 | 2 | 3 | 4 | 5 | 6 | 7 | 8 | 9 | 10 |
|---|---|---|---|---|---|---|---|---|---|----|

**Not**
**Confidence**                                                  **Extremely**
                                                                **Confidence**

**Please explain your answer.**

_______________________________________________________________

_______________________________________________________________

_______________________________________________________________

_______________________________________________________________

# SELF-CARE

**We care about others and easily forget about ourselves. Self-care is care provided by you to yourself. You need to identify your beneficial needs and wants, and fulfill your desires and wishes. You need to assure yourself that you are healthy physically, mentally, emotionally, and spiritually.**

**You need to connect with nature, write a card to a love one, get a massage, meditate in your favorite place, exercise regularly, breath fresh and clean air, listen to music, enjoy a great book, watch a good movie, have fun, spoil yourself with things you can afford, energize yourself with a balanced diet, sleep well, take a nap and rest your body and mind, learn something new, and spend time with true friends who make you laugh.**

1.  Have you neglected your self-care? YES/NO. Please elaborate.

_______________________________________________________________

_______________________________________________________________

_______________________________________________________________

_______________________________________________________________

2.  When was the last time you have done something for yourself? Please elaborate.

_______________________________________________________________

_______________________________________________________________

_______________________________________________________________

_______________________________________________________________

3.  Have you cared for others and neglected yourself? YES/NO. Please elaborate.

_______________________________________________________________

_______________________________________________________________

_______________________________________________________________

_______________________________________________________________

4.  How do you describe the behaviors that made you care less about yourself?

_______________________________________________________________

_______________________________________________________________

_______________________________________________________________

_______________________________________________________________

_______________________________________________________________

5.  What can you do to increase self-care?

 

 

6.  Please list the people, things, and places that you care about. Why?

 

 

7.  Have you neglected yourself in order to care about others? YES/NO. Please explain.

 

 

8.  When was the last time you visited your primary doctor? _______________
9.  When was the last time you visited your dentist? _______________
10. When was the last time you had a massage? _______________
11. When was the last time you spoiled yourself? _______________
12. When was the last time you laughed and had fun? _______________
13. When was the last time you felt good about yourself? _______________
14. When was the last time you loved being you? _______________
15. When was the last time you smiled at a stranger? _______________
16. When was the last time you were able to relax and feel peace? _______________
17. When was the last time you felt positive about yourself? _______________

**18. How much do you love and care about yourself NOW? Please circle one.**

| **0** | **1** | **2** | **3** | **4** | **5** | **6** | **7** | **8** | **9** | **10** | **+** |
|---|---|---|---|---|---|---|---|---|---|---|---|

**Do not**
**Love or Care**                                                                 **Extremely Love & Care**

Please reflect about your answer.

 

 

# HEALING WHEN JOURNALING

**I encourage you to journal every day. Journaling has a charming effect.**

**Healing may use reflection and mindfulness observations by seeking words to describe our goals, strengths, weakness, thoughts, feelings, actions, and attitudes. We may write about our pains, ambitions and dreams, aggressively, patiently or sensitively on paper. Paper takes all types of ink, and any color. We may express our ability to perceive and process our inner selves by constructing awareness of life experiences. We may conclude ideas and re-build self-esteem, self-confidence, and self-determination by reactivating memories and recreating positive and less positive moments. We will teach ourselves by journaling. We may heal, learn, organize, transform, change, create, meditate, recall, imagine, improve, build, re-build, and restore our lives by journaling.**

**My Journal:**

_______________________________________________________

_______________________________________________________

_______________________________________________________

_______________________________________________________

_______________________________________________________

_______________________________________________________

_______________________________________________________

_______________________________________________________

_______________________________________________________

_______________________________________________________

_______________________________________________________

_______________________________________________________

_______________________________________________________

_______________________________________________________

_______________________________________________________

_______________________________________________________

# DAILY ANGER METER

**Today is a good day.**

**Today is** _______________________________

**Date:** _______________________________

**What was the highest number you reached on the anger meter today?**

- **How angry were you today?**

| 0 | 1 | 2 | 3 | 4 | 5 | 6 | 7 | 8 | 9 | 10 | + |
|---|---|---|---|---|---|---|---|---|---|----|---|

No Anger                    Extremely Angry

1.  **What was the event that triggered your highest number on the anger meter?**

    _______________________________________________

    _______________________________________________

    _______________________________________________

2.  **What would you have done different?** _______________________

    _______________________________________________

    _______________________________________________

    _______________________________________________

3.  **Were you able to pause, and apply assertiveness coping skills? YES/NO Please explain.**

    _______________________________________________

4.  **Did you apply self-control? YES/NO** _______________________

5.  **Please write the signs that you were able to identify when you felt angry:**

    **Physical signs:** _______________________________________
    **Mental signs:** _______________________________________
    **Emotional signs:** _______________________________________
    **Behavioral signs:** _______________________________________

**Comments:** _______________________________________

_______________________________________________

_______________________________________________

*Reflect and discuss your daily events and comments in group and with your psychotherapist. Make copies of this blank sheet and use it daily.*

# WEEKLY ANGER METER

**Today is a good day.**

**Week from:** _____________________ **To:** _________________

**What was the highest number you reached on the anger meter this week?**

| **0** | **1** | **2** | **3** | **4** | **5** | **6** | **7** | **8** | **9** | **10** | **+** |
|---|---|---|---|---|---|---|---|---|---|---|---|
| No Anger | | | | | | | | | | | Extremely Angry |

_____   _____   _____   _____   _____   _____   _____
  M      T      W     TH     F      S      S

**What happened? Please elaborate.**

**Monday:** _______________________________________________

**Tuesday:** ______________________________________________

**Wednesday:** ____________________________________________

**Thursday:** _____________________________________________

**Friday:** _______________________________________________

**Saturday:** _____________________________________________

**Sunday:** _______________________________________________

1.  **What was the event that triggered the highest number?**

    _______________________________________________________

    _______________________________________________________

2.  **What would you have done different?** _______________________

    _______________________________________________________

3.  **Please write the signs that you were able to identify when you felt angry:**

**Physical signs:** _______________________________________

**Mental signs:** _________________________________________

**Emotional signs:** ______________________________________

**Behavioral signs:** _____________________________________

*Reflect and discuss your weekly and daily events and comments in group and with your psychotherapist. Make copies of this blank sheet and use it weekly.*

# CONTRACT

I, _________________________________________________ agree to learn and

demonstrate knowledge of application of anger management coping skills, including self-control.

_________ (initials) I agree to care for myself, to eat well, and to get enough sleep each night.

_________ (initials) I agree to complete my daily and weekly anger meter sheets.

_________ (initials) I agree to utilize my social support and community resources.

_________ (initials) I agree that, if I need help I will contact the following individuals:

_______________________________________________________________

_______________________________________________________________

_______________________________________________________________

_________ (initials) I agree to learn and demonstrate knowledge of application of problem

solving, decision making, conflict resolution, and healthy communication coping

skills.

_________ (initials) I agree to pause and wisely reflect before reacting.

_________ (initials) I agree to the following conditions: _______________________________

_______________________________________________________________

_______________________________________________________________

_______________________________________________________________

_________ (initials) I agree that these conditions are important, and worth following.

_________ (initials) I agree that this is a contract that I am willing to follow.

_________ (initials) I agree to honor this contract.

Signed_______________________________________________Date______________

Witnessed by_________________________________________Date______________

# FEEDBACK

**Please send me your suggestions, questions, observations, and comments. You may assist us in improving future publications. We are open to constructive criticism and appreciate your experience and insight.**

**Thank you.**

**Please contact me at rlima001@gmail.com**

**Please rate this workbook.**

| 0 | 1 | 2 | 3 | 4 | 5 | 6 | 7 | 8 | 9 | 10 |
|---|---|---|---|---|---|---|---|---|---|----|
| Terrible | | | | | | | | | | Great |

**Please elaborate:**

_______________________________________________

_______________________________________________

_______________________________________________

_______________________________________________

_______________________________________________

_______________________________________________

**Suggestions:**

_______________________________________________

_______________________________________________

_______________________________________________

_______________________________________________

_______________________________________________

_______________________________________________

_______________________________________________

_______________________________________________

_______________________________________________

# NOTES

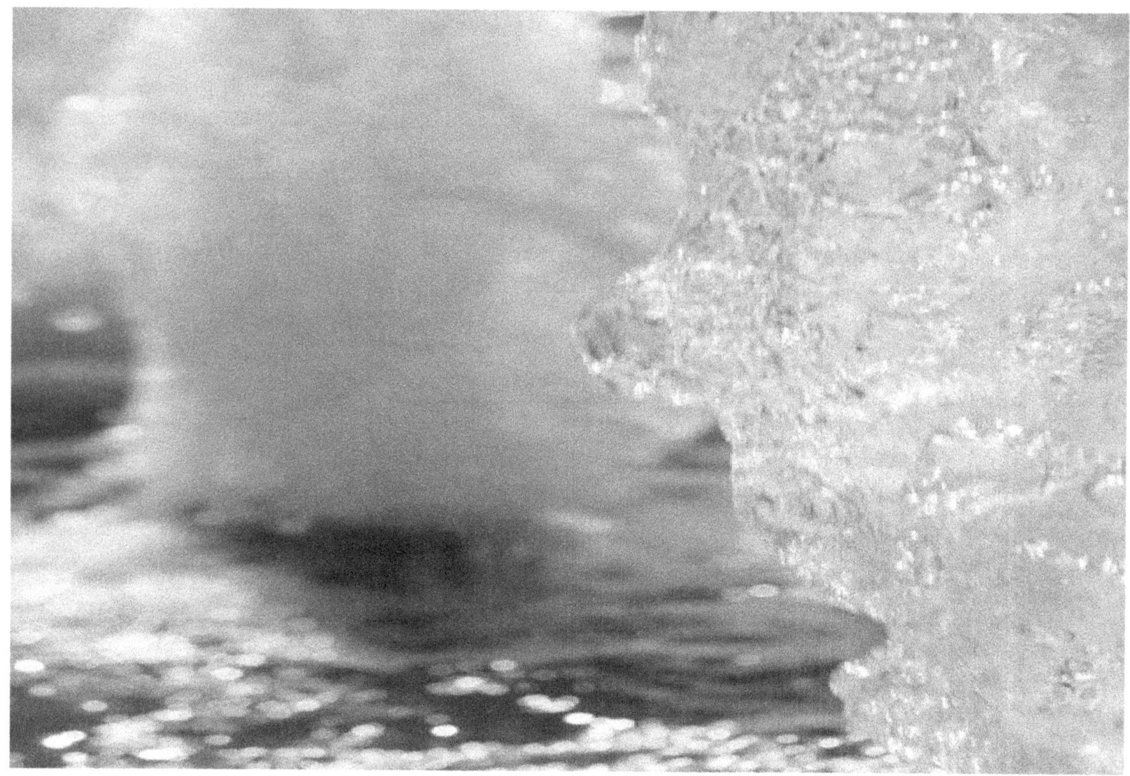

# BE LIKE WATER

Water does not fight its way but finds a way. If you drop an open bottle of water on the floor, the water will not break the floor. The water will go around and into everything until it finds its destiny in a soft and calm way.

Adjusting to everything is a sublime experience. Accepting first that life is unfair is true awareness. Deciding to become part of your blue print or destiny is genuine understanding of your life purpose.

 Increasing self-responsibility and self-accountability helps master and acquire self-determination. You are the shape of your thoughts and your actions are the results of such process.

No more blaming, no more excuses, no more denial, no more justification, rationalizations, or minimizations. No more fakeness or lies. Apply what you know to be beneficial to you, and to what you love and care.

**The wind challenges the anger of a naked tree
standing cold, calm,
and free**